PAGAN

G000255109

Land Of ᴛʜᴇ ɢᴏᴅᴅᴇss

CHERYL STRAFFON

Introduction by **MONICA SJÖÖ**

Illustrations by **Geraldine Andrew,
Su Bayfield, Gabrielle Hawkes, Rose Lewis,
Caeia March, Marjorianne Rowland, Monica Sjöö.**

MEYN MAMVRO PUBLICATIONS

Pagan Cornwall – Land of the Goddess

By Cheryl Straffon

First published in 1993 by Meyn Mamvro Publications,
51 Carn Bosavern, St. Just, Penzance, Cornwall TR19 7QX.
Printed by Headland Printers, Penzance, Cornwall
Reprinted 1995, 1997, 2000, 2004.

ISBN: 0 9518859 2 8

THE AUTHOR
Cheryl Straffon is editor of the Cornish pagan-oriented earth mysteries
magazine "Meyn Mamvro" and author of 4 guides to the ancient sites in West
Penwith, Bodmin Moor & North Cornwall, Mid-Cornwall & the Lizard, and
The Isles of Scilly. She is also author of "Fentynyow Kernow – in search of
Cornwall's Holy Wells" and Megalithic Mysteries of Cornwall". She lives
and works near the sea and the moors in West Penwith.

*Front Cover photograph is of Boleigh fogou in Springtime [c] Cheryl Straffon.
Other picture and artwork credits are on p.116.*

CONTENTS

NOTE

Dates are given in BCE (Before Common Era) and CE (Common Era), being equivalent to the former BC & AD respectively.

References to books and publications are listed at the end of each chapter. Where there is a specific quotation or item referred to, the page number of the source is given. Where no such page number is given, the reference refers to the whole book or publication.

PREFACE

From the waters of the river Tamar, named after a goddess Tamara, to the Isles of Scilly, named perhaps after a goddess Sillina, Cornwall has been, and in many ways still is, a land apart from the rest of England. As a child, I used to look from my bedroom window across the Tamar herself into Devon; and as an adult I have looked from my bedroom window across to the Isles of Scilly. From one end of Cornwall to another I have journeyed, always aware of the special separate quality of the land. For each individual person there will be different reasons why Cornwall is so special and different, but for me it is because I can feel the ancient ways and the sacred land still alive in a way I feel nowhere else. Those ancient ways and that sacred land take me to the heart of the mystery known as The Goddess, a spiritual essence who was once revered, loved and acknowledged in this land, and whose ways lingered on here perhaps later than many other places.

Many books have been written on ancient Cornwall, but for me they have generally lacked the insight that the land and its peoples was, and in many ways still is, the children of the life-giving and sustaining force of the universe, known to our Paleolithic, Neolithic, Bronze Age and Celtic ancestors as The Goddess. This book then is my small attempt to reclaim her again, to find her rightful place in the land that is hers. In the process many interesting nuggets from the past have emerged, some already known but not linked together before, others perhaps forgotten or their significance overlooked. But always it was the awareness of her presence in my country and in my heart that led me on, and will, I hope, lead you on to find her again in the pages of this book and in Cornwall herself – land of the Goddess.

The book has one major premise – that there was a continuity of tradition that was often altered, modified or transformed, but nevertheless had a consistent thread from the earliest times up until the present day. This premise may not be accepted by some researchers, but nevertheless much of the new archaeological and mythological study has shown that this is a reasonable and sustainable premise upon which to work. The pace of change was much slower for our predecessors, and many hundreds if not thousands of years would pass without any major alteration in the rhythms of life. In this connection, I owe a great debt to the ground-breaking work done by Marija Gimbutas and others in the women's spirituality study movement, and I am pleased to be able to apply the results of their diligent research to my own land of Cornwall. Although some of the suggestions in this book are tentative and speculative, nevertheless they are all founded on a matrix of material research and evidence. In particular, the first chapter lays down the overview of the prehistoric celebration of the Goddess to which all the material in the subsequent chapters should be related back.

That material is taken from current research in archaeology, mythology, folklore, legend, and earth mysteries, and if I have inadvertently overlooked a reference to source or an acknowledgement it is because 3 years of reading and talking to people sometimes makes you forget where an idea first sprang from! Six years of editing the Cornish earth mysteries/pagan magazine "Meyn Mamvro" (Cornish for 'Stones of our Motherland') has been a tremendous priviledge and inestimable help in gathering and collating material relating to the book, and I would like to thank all the contributors for the well of material into which I have dipped from time to time for suggestions and promptings. (Specifically, some of chapters 4, 5 & 7 have already appeared by me in previous "Meyn Mamvros").

I would especially like to give thanks for the help freely given me by Monica Sjöö, a Goddess-celebrating and woman-supporting writer who provided the introduction and the chapter illustrations. My thanks also to other artists in Cornwall whose original work accompanies the text, specifically Marjorianne Rowland, Gabrielle Hawkes, Caeia March, Geraldine Andrew, Rose Lewis and Su Bayfield. I would also like to acknowledge those members of my Goddess-celebrating ritual group Lor-Hag-Mor (Cornish for 'moon and sea') with whom I worked for 3 years, and to the members of various womens full moon groups with whom I have shared many wonderful rituals. This book was written during a time of great personal change for me, and above all I would like to thank Caeia for her loving encouragement, her consistent enthusiasm and her fine editing work on my text. I only hope it now does the Goddess credit.

Cheryl Straffon
Imbolc 1993.

INTRODUCTION

by MONICA SJÖÖ

I first met Cheryl Straffon at the Ley Hunter Moot held in September 1990 at CAER in Lamorna. I had been invited to give a slide-presentation of the Goddess in my paintings inspired by journeys and experiences at Her sacred sites in these isles. Cheryl gave a presentation of "Earth Mysteries in West Penwith". It would have to have been the first time that such Goddess-celebrating women as Cheryl and myself had participated as major speakers at such an event as this Moot. I had been nervous to come since my relationship with the male-dominated Earth Mysteries movement had been fraught, to say the least, over a number of years. I have always had a kind of love/hate relationship to this movement, but at the same time I see myself as an integral part of it. I have been inspired by it and angered by it from the very start.

I had been aware of it since the 60s, and it seemed at the time most so-called Earth Mysteries researchers simply didn't want to recognise that the Neolithic, when so many of the sacred sites were created, was a time without priestly male hierarchies, caste systems and kingship. Then as now there was a great resistance against recognising that just possibly collectives of powerful creative women, who were the ancient farmers, healers, scientists and psychics, were the initiators of those ancient cultures. They formed them in their own image and that of their beloved Great Mother of the Heavens, Earth and the Under/Other world.

The Palaeolithic Mountain Mother, the Mother Ancestor of the animals to the peoples of the caves, had shapeshifted in truly shamanic ways into Corn Mother, serpentine waters, radiant Moon in the nightsky, and maternal lifegiving Sun in the daysky. She was still the Mother of the Spirits who is both dark and light. Presumably it was women's magic understandings that brought into being the megalithic culture of the living stones, the Moon and waters, that Marija Gimbutas explores so thoroughly in her books: "The Language of the Goddess", and "The Civilisation of the Goddess", both published in recent years.

6

I wrote the first draft of what was over the years to become "The Great Cosmic Mother" book already in 1975, and one of the impulses for writing it at the time was my frustrations with what I saw as the denial of the Goddess and women's ancient wisdom – women who communicated with me at the time in visions and dreams and through my paintings – in the Earth Mysteries movement. In 1976 however I came across Guy Underwood's book "Patterns of the Past", and the next year Michael Dames' books "Silbury Treasure: the Great Goddess rediscovered", and "Avebury Circle" were published. These books were to change the course of my life, and after a visionary journey of trance experiences in an altered state at Silbury, Avebury and West Kennett long barrow in February 1978, I finally "knew" the Goddess of the land and she became utterly real to me.

I knew that Earth is our living and creating Mother and I experienced vividly her great pain and grief and the danger all biological life now faces at this time. Patriarchal genetic engineers and nuclear physicists, and the Western-led "New World Order" they work for, could annihilate all life as we know it. We must now dream alive the past and future and we must return to the Mother if we want to live. In our dreams we link with the Neolithic shamanwomen who still coexist with us in other realms, and in more recent times we reconnect with the Wise women who were burnt at the stake for being powerfully sexually, psychically and magically female.

It was those experiences in an altered state at Silbury and Avebury in 1978 that led me to pilgrimage ever since to the sacred places of the Mother, and I went to live in a small hamlet near Fishguard in Celtic Pembrokeshire, so similar to West Penwith in Celtic Cornwall, where I explored the many beautiful Neolithic and Celtic remains as well as sacred wells and trees. I lived there during five years and in my dreams I still dwell there.

All of this is the background why I personally so much welcome this book about the Goddess in Cornwall, especially since it is written by someone so central to the Earth Mysteries movement. On the second day of the Ley Hunter Moot we set off (by coach) on what was billed as "The Old Stones of Land End Ley Trip" to be led by John Michell and Cheryl Straffon. Our journey took us to the Merry Maidens, Boscawen-un and Tregeseal stone circles, as well as quoits and standing stones in fields.

I never forgot how refreshing it was to have Cheryl, giving her explanations of the sites, firmly rooted in her knowledge of ancient women's lunar wisdom ways. It gave us all a manysided and allrounded view of the past.

An exciting aspect of this book is that Cheryl is not only well versed in the Earth Mysteries research but she has also a wealth of knowledge of local legends, stories and mythology. This is important material when one is attempting to piece together what was and is the meaning to local people of the many sites that so abound all over Cornwall, but especially in West Penwith. I gather that Cromwell and his puritans never made much of an impression on Cornwall and that this is one reason why such awesome events such as the Padstow "Obby Oss" celebration on Mayday or Beltane has always been a living tradition. I went to Padstow the first Beltane (in 1986) after the death of my young son and I found the death and rebirth theme, the black horse dancing through the streets, and the drum music absolutely moving and haunting. Life would not be worth living without real traditions such as these that connect us with the past and our Ancestors who live on in other realms.

I would like to thank Cheryl for keeping our memories alive and piecing together some of the mystery. This book will be inspiring and useful to women everywhere, and also to men who love and cherish Earth our Mother.

Monica Sjöö
February 1993.

MONICA SJÖÖ is internationally renouned as co-author of "The Great Cosmic Mother" (1987), a widely-respected work on Goddess cultures, & author of "New Age and Armageddon" (1992), an analysis of the 'New Age' in society today. She has had numerous exhibitions of her Goddess paintings, and regularly facilitates workshops and slide presentations. Some of her artwork can be found at the beginning of each chapter of this book.

CORNWALL

Places mentioned in the text

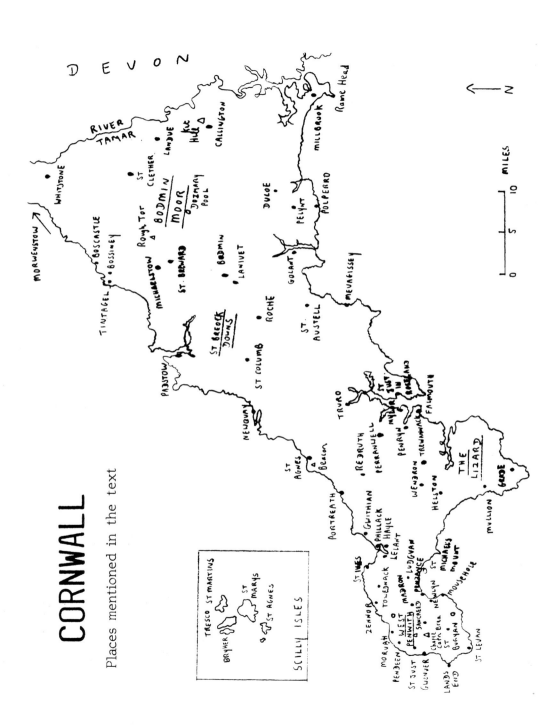

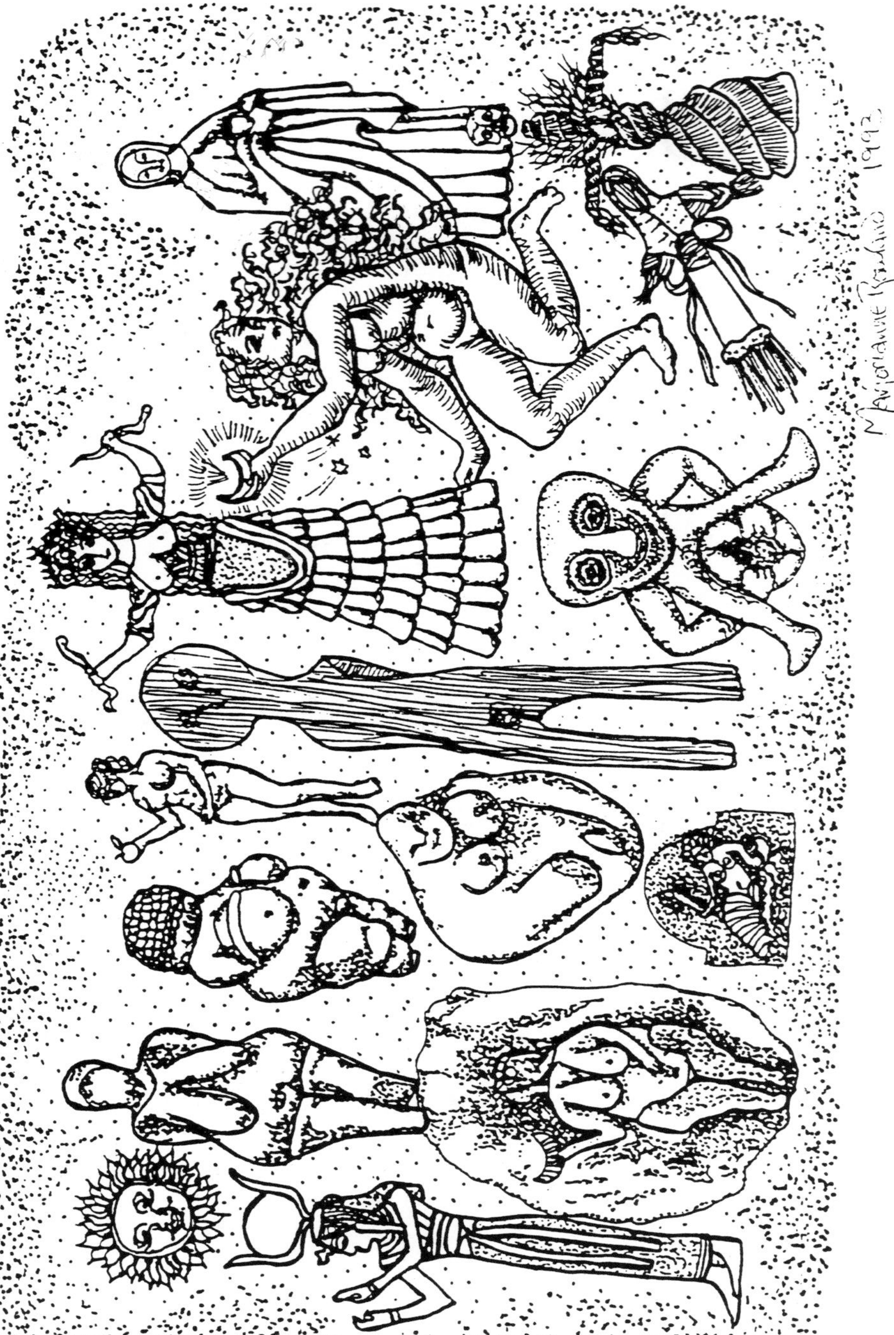
1993

The Goddess was revered, acknowledged and celebrated throughout the world for at least 20,000 years, a vast aeon of time before the rise of the patriarchal religions such as Judeaism, Christianity and Islam: these have only been a blip on the horizon of the last 2000 or so years, though in many ways a devastating one. Archaeological and mythological research increasingly shows that there was a long continuity of tradition from the earliest remains of humankind right up to the present day, and the story of the Goddess is the story of the creative source of all life as she was celebrated for thousands of years before being driven underground or assimilated into the new dominator religions. The story is remarkably similar throughout the world, although there were different processes of change in different places. The story of Cornwall fits into the matrix of European pre-history, so the spiritual beliefs and their expressions by the people of the land that came to be called Cornwall need to be seen in the wider context of the European stage.

The earliest human remains in Europe are those found in 1960 in a cave at Petralona in Northern Greece. Traces of fire used by humans there have been dated to approx. 700,000 BCE, and it is known from elsewhere that fire was originally used by women in a protective and ritual magic way.[1] Also in the cave a completely preserved human skull dating between 700,000 – 2000,000 BCE was found: the person was aged about 35 years and may have been deliberately buried in a ceremonial way as the oldest person of the community, 35 years being a very good age at that time. To enter the cave where it was found is an awesome feeling: it is a vast beautiful place full of stalactites and stalagmites, which are known from elsewhere to have been seen by the cave-dwellers as sacred to the mother goddess.[2]

Caves were very special places to our Paleolithic ancestors – the hunter-gatherers who at certain times in their following of the migratory herds would stay in the caves in small communities. Such caves have been discovered in northern Spain and south-west France and have revealed, over the last 100 years since their discovery, the most amazing decorations that have revolutionised our approaches to these ancient peoples. From about 30,000 to 10,000 BCE these caves seem to have been sacred dwellings of the Goddess, and they were perhaps perceived as the body of the Goddess herself, the actual hollow shape symbolising her "all-containing womb, which brought forth the living and took back the dead."[3] On the walls in the innermost sanctity of the caves at Lascaux, Les Trois Frerès and others are painted images of animals and shamans in which the figures that have been interpreted as female ones occupy central place. This interpretation is reinforced by the discovery outside certain caves and rock shelters of carvings of Goddess figures, such as the Goddess of Laussal and the Goddess of Lespugue. The Goddess of Laussal, who dates from about 20,000 BCE, carries a bisons horn in her right hand, shaped like the crescent of the moon with 13 notations representing the 13 months of the lunar year, a very early identification of the Goddess with the moon. The Goddess of Lespugue, dating from the same period, was carved from the ivory of a mammoth and emphasises her breasts and buttocks, a Goddess of birth and nourishment.

Other Paleolithic carvings of the Goddess from the same period (about 20,000 BCE) have been found in other areas of Europe: for example, the Goddess of Willendorf in Austria [right] made from limestone, with her emphasis on the breast, belly and womb, and the Pavlov figurines from Dolní Vestonice in old Czechoslovakia with their focus on the breasts and swelling hips. These images all concentrate on the fertility of the primal Mother Goddess, the giver and nourisher of life. Other more abstract carvings focus on the genital triangle and are covered with meanders and chevrons (diamond shapes):

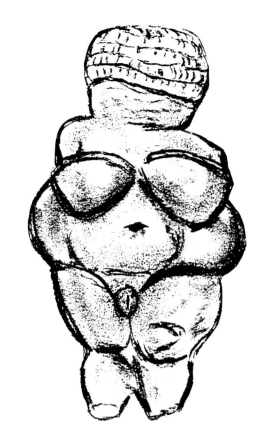

there are more than a hundred images of the vulva from paleolithic France, showing that the Goddess was recognised as a giver of birth. To date no similar specific images of the male form have been found, and from this we can conclude that the Goddess was worshipped as the life-giving, sustaining and renewing force of the universe. Burial sites at Mal'ta in Siberia, as well as producing hundreds of carved figures have elicited skeletons of a 4 year old child, lying in the foetal position facing east to the rising sun, the body decorated and the grave coloured red, the colour of the life-blood itself. A similar burial where the body was painted red was found in the Paviland Cave near Bristol in SW Britain, showing that the practice was widespread throughout the prehistoric world. There are traces of the Paleolithic peoples in the other caves of Britain too, such as Kent's Cavern, Windmill Hill cavern and Lower Tornewton Cave in

Devon, and it seems likely that other caves would have been similarly occupied in Cornwall, the evidence for which is now buried or washed away. Some Paleolithic remains however have been found at Gwithian on the NW Cornish coast.

The Goddess then was the wholeness of all, and all animals, creatures, plants and stones, women and men were part of her unity. She governed the cycles of life, death and rebirth, and wherever we find images and symbols of her, the cave paintings of animals, the abstract designs, or the carvings of the moon, birds, fish and wild animals, we see her numinosity represented. As Marija Gimbutas says: "The primordial deity for our Paleolithic and Neolithic ancestors was female... no images have been found of a Father God throughout the prehistoric record."[4] We can therefore surmise that the same mythological view of the Goddess prevailed in Britain as well as in other parts of Europe.

As the Paleolithic became the Mesolithic and Neolithic era (10,000 BCE – 3000 BCE approx.) the climate improved, and the hunter-gatherers, having by now discovered agriculture, began to settle in small communities, cultivating the soil, domesticating and breeding animals, weaving cloth and making pottery. As Monica Sjöö & Barbara Mor have shown[5], these activities were all likely to have been the province of women who had every reason to continue their love of the Mother Goddess in providing the tribe with all its abundance and stability. This was a time of great harmony and co-operation. There are, as Reinne Eisler points out[6], no images found from this period of warfare or agression, no remains of spears, swords or other instruments of killing, no burials of chieftans or war-leaders, no pictures that celebrate or even depict warfare, but rather a myriad of images and forms depicting life, continuity, growth, fertility and equality.

A wealth of carvings have been found from this period, many of which show Goddesses of fecundity and fruitfulness, such as the Lady of Pazardzik from central Bulgaria (4500 BCE approx.), a Goddess of life, death, and rebirth. Spiral images of the moon, of the cosmic egg, of heads of bird-women and serpent-goddesses, and the grain-goddesses of vegetation and fertility all appear. Sometimes she is imaged as the Lady of the Beasts, and her form appears, among others, as a bird, a lion, a fish, a bull, a dog, a bee and a butterfly. The butterfly shape was later to evolve into the labrys or double-headed axe, a symbol that was originally a peaceful manifestation of the

Goddess. Many of the Neolithic axes that have been found throughout Europe (and Cornwall was one of the principal exporters of axes during this period) are clearly not weapons, but ritualistic ornaments, the axe functioning as a symbol of Goddess regeneration.[7]

From the Meditteranean in the south, to Romania, Hungary and Poland in the north, from the Black Sea in the east to Germany in the west, an area Marija Gimbutas has called Old Europe[8], and from where Neolithic tribes probably journeyed to Britain, the evidence of a rich and advanced Goddess-worshipping civilisation has emerged. Some 30,000 miniature sculptures made of clay, marble bone, copper and gold have been discovered in some 3000 sites, including the amazing discoveries at Çatal Hüyük in Turkey, and the Vinca culture in Yugoslavia. At Çatal Hüyük the central figure in one decorated shrine room after another was the Mother Goddess who appears in 3 aspects, as a young woman, a mother giving birth, and an old woman. It has been suggested by archaeologist James Mellaart, who excavated the site, that the religion may have been the creation of women who elaborated a mythology where the birth-giving and nourishing capacity of the Goddess image was emphasised. Twin-goddess figures appear in several shrine rooms, and some of these figures are also found in Vinca and other places. Some of the figures of the Goddess were placed in graves, a ritual that linked together the cycles of life, death and rebirth, a practice that still continued until quite recent times in parts of rural Greece.[9]

These double-headed figures with 2 pairs of breasts but only one set of arms may represent mother and maiden, or they may be sister Goddesses, or perhaps women-loving Goddesses. Carvings such as chevrons, meanders and zig-zags continue to appear, and are now widely found on pottery throughout Neolithic Europe, including Britain and Cornwall (such as the Neolithic beaker found at Trevedra near St Just-in-Penwith in 1954) [right].[10]

Towards the end of this period (5000 – 2500 BCE approx.) the Minoan Goddess–celebrating civilisation flowered in Crete, and the great Megalithic culture arose in Western Europe, with its Goddess temples on Malta, its Goddess carvings and spirals in the tombs of Brittany and Ireland, and its great stone circles in Britain which were often aligned to a landscape perceived as a living Goddess (see Chapter 2 for more details). The same ritual structures and images of the Goddess are found in places as far apart as Britain, Malta, Old Europe, Anatolia, Syria and the Indus Valley. The Goddess was everywhere and everything: she was not just part of life, she was life itself, and as Marija Gimbutas says: "The Goddess in all her manifestations was the symbol of the unity of all life in Nature. Her power was in water and stone, in tomb and cave, in animals and birds, snakes and fish, hills, trees and flowers. Hence the holistic and mythopoeic perception of the sacredness and mystery of all there is on earth."[11]

The societies that celebrated this all–embracing Goddess for 20,000 or so years were probably matrifocal rather than matriarchal, that is, women–orientated rather than female-dominating, for the evidence points to an egalitarian and co-operative society that honoured and revered the female qualities. But while these societies existed in the area of what we now know as Europe and the Near East, to the north a very different kind of society was gathering strength. These were the nomadic tribesmen from the steppelands of eastern Russia, traditionally called Indo–European, but named by Gimbutas as Kurgan. These agressively patriarchal peoples wielded the battle–axe and the dagger, rode horses expertly, and worshipped not a Goddess of the Earth, but Gods of the sky and thunder. They were war–like, hierarchal people, and when they invaded Old Europe in 3 waves (4300–4200 BCE, 3400–3200 BCE, & 3000–2800 BCE) they all but obliterated the peaceful Goddess–loving culture. The course of history was irreparably altered, and the spiritual ethos of the people was forcibly changed from a gynocentric, goddess–loving one to a subjugated war–orientated patriarchal one.

However, the process, although devastating for the subsequent history of humankind, was not immediate nor complete. In some places, usually the further reaches of the European area, the effect was tempered by the presence of the native religions, and this has implications for Britain and Cornwall, on the far western fringes of Europe. The Bronze Age in Britain (2500–1000 BCE approx.) was characterised by a continuation of the megalithic building of the Neolithic, although the type of burial changed, and the focus of worship probably also changed. The Goddess was still celebrated, but now she became divided, and existed in relationship to a male God who became her son and her consort, in an eternal cycle of life that reflected the agricultral/pastoral society of the Bronze Age peoples. The orientation of some of the megalithic monuments changed from that of the moon to that of the sun, who was probably originally a goddess, part of the complete whole of the Goddess, but by now may have been changing to a God who existed in relationship to the Earth Mother. It is also from this period that emerged the great mythic cycle of the Goddess – the wheel of the year – and her relationship to the solar gods, who gain their nourishment from her and are eventually sacrificed to ensure her continued fertility. This concept has survived through 2000 years of a very different religion – Christianity – and has re-emerged in the 20th century as the basis of neo-paganism.

At another fringe of Europe – Crete – something parallel was also happening. The great Minoan civilisation of Crete had been a comparitively late (3000–1250 BCE) Goddess-celebrating culture, and some of the most beaut-iful Goddess figurines date from this period, inclucing the famous Minoan snake goddesses [right]. The cult sites of Knossos, Phaestos and Malia on Crete have been excavated and shown to be ritual centres for the celebration of the Goddess, symbols of whom included birds, bees, double axes, and in particular the bull and the labyrinth or maze.

There are no images of gods until later, when the Minoan peoples of Crete established contact with the Myceneans on the mainland (1600–1450 BCE). These were the same peoples who had come from the Indo European/Kurgan invasions mentioned previously, but here they seem to have existed in peaceful co-operation with the Minoans until a further wave of invasions (1150 BCE) destroyed the civilisation. During this period of co-operation the Goddess-celebrating culture of the Minoans was fused with the God-centered religion of the Myceneans to produce a harmonious culture of the Goddess and her consort-son, which later became reversed and depreciated into the ruling Gods of the Greek pantheon with their Goddess consorts.

It is from this Mycenean–Minoan period that interestingly we find links between Greece and Cornwall. A bronze dagger found at Pelynt in Cornwall in the late 19th century of unknown provenance, but possibly discovered in a barrow, is undoubtedly Mycenean in origin. It shows striking parallels with daggers or short swords made c1300–1230 BCE in the Mycenean–Minoan area, and is evidence of possible trade and contact between Cornwall and Greece at this period. In addition a tin ingot dredged from Falmouth Harbour about 1810 has also been considered to have typological affinities with an East Mediterranean type of metal ingot of the second millennium BCE, and might therefore be used to support the argument of a connection between the Aegean Bronze Age and Cornish tin resources.[12] The Goddess-worshipping peoples of the Mediterranean may therefore have been known to the peoples of the south-west peninsula of Britain, and vice-versa, and their respective religious beliefs, if not the same,

must also have been mutually cognisant. Another intriguing find, which may date from the same period, was a bronze bull found at St Just-in-Penwith in 1832, which was attributed to the Phoenicians at the time,[13] but which may have come from the eastern Meditteranean, bearing in mind the significance of the bull cult in Minoan Crete.

The Iron Age (1000 BCE approx.) marked the further rise of the worship of the sky gods and with it tribal warfare and internecine conflict. It was the time of the building of the great hill forts in Cornwall, such as Carn Brea and Trencrom Hill. But it was also the time when the courtyard house settlements were constructed and people continued to live in small agricultural communities, their lives inseparably wedded to the great round of the year's cycle. In religious terms, there probably continued to be a movement away from the idea of the Goddess as spiritual essence of the universe towards a concept of the sun–god as a more separate son–consort of the Goddess herself. But change in remote and rural areas was always slow, and this would have applied particularly to Cornwall. For Cornwall began to develop during this period the unique fogous – underground chambers – which may well have been used for ritual purposes to continue to celebrate the power of the Goddess, who, by now, may have been identified primarily as an Earth Goddess (see Chapter 2). Other special places in the land were noted for their numinosity or manisfestation of her power (see Chapter 3), in particular wells, which were especially thought of as sacred places for communion with her (see Chapter 4).

Iron Age society in Cornwall, as in Ireland, Wales, Scotland, Mann and Brittany, was a Celtic one, and this has definite implications for the continuation of Goddess worship. For the Celts were a people given to religion, art and writing, and they preserved and continued much of the culture of their forebears. The Goddess continued to be celebrated, although by now she had become split into various goddesses and gods (see Chapter 6), many of whom were tribal deities and each of whom had different functions. With the coming of Christianity and the establishment of the One God, the Goddess had nowhere to go but underground. She could not be eliminated, for the principle of the female as the central spiritual force of the universe can never be eliminated, but there was little room for her in the Christian dogma which perverted her act of continuing creation, life, death and rebirth, into one where she did not even have a part to play! The people however continued to love her, and certainly, in the early days of Celtic Christianity, her functions were often transferred to the Celtic saints and later re–emerged in the legends of the Matter of Britain, including the Welsh Triads, the Arthurian cycle, and, specifically for Cornwall, the story of Tristan and Iseult (see Chapter 6).

Meanwhile, in the particular agricultural-pastoral community that was Dumnonia, and that part of it which was to become Kernow (Cornwall), the great mythic cycle of the Goddess continued to be celebrated in the season's round of festivals and events, many of which had become only nominally Christian (see Chapter 7). By the Middle Ages the Goddess had all but been forgotten as a focus of worship, as Christianity had reinforced its iron grip over the centuries, but nevertheless many of the old ways of manifesting her magic through spells and hedge lore continued to be practised by the village wise-women and white witches right up until the early years of the 20th century (see Chapter 8). Her eclipse was but brief, for like the moon who wanes and then disappears only for a few dark days, she has reappeared again at the end of the 20th century in the enormous revival of interest in her faith among present day neo-pagans (see Chapter 9).

And so the Goddess has been ever-present in Cornwall for as long as human beings have lived here. Her form and function have changed and metamorphasised over that vast span of time, and yet through all the changes her quintessential power has remained and been manifested, either openly or occluded. So let us embark on a journey of discovery and see where we may find her in her sacred land of Cornwall.

BIBLIOGRAPHY
1. "Lady of the Beasts" – Buffie Johnson (p21) [Harper Collins, 1990]
2. "Lady of the Beasts" – Buffie Johnson (p44) [Harper Collins 1990]
3. "Myth of the Goddess" –Anne Baring & Jules Cashford (p16) [Penguin 1991]
4. "The Civilisation of the Goddess" – Marija Gimbutas (pX) [Harper 1991]
5. "The Great Cosmic Mother" –Monica Sjöö & Barbara Mor (p33) [Harper 1987]
6. "The Chalice and the Blade" – Riane Eisler (p17–21) [Pandora 1993]
7. "The Civilisation of the Goddess" – Marija Gimbutas (p209) [Harper 1991]
8. "Goddesses and Gods of Old Europe" – Marija Gimbutas [ThamesHudson 1982]
9. "Lesbos; an ancient pagan isle" – Cheryl Straffon [The Cauldron 58 1990]
10. "Archaeology of South-West Britain" – Susan Pearce (p59) [Collins 1981]
11. "Language of the Goddess" – Marija Gimbutas (p321) [ThamesHudson 1989]
12. "A glance at Cornish Tin" – Stuart Piggott [from "Ancient Europe and the Mediterranean" (p142) [Aris & Philips 1977]
13. "St Just" – Rev. Buller (p6) [Rodda 1842]

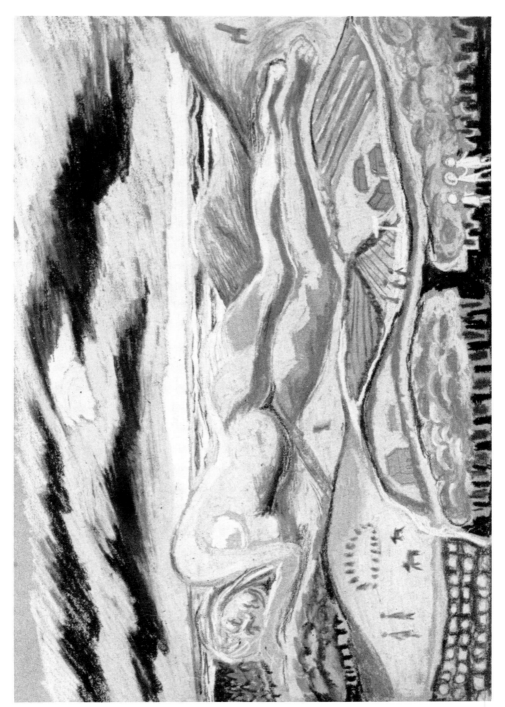

CHAPTER 2   SITES OF THE GODDESS

        To ancient peoples the earth was a living being, and
every rock, animal, tree, flower and fruit imbued with the same
spirit that flowed through women and men. She was also an
aspect of the Goddess, their mother who nurtured and sustained
the tribe and as such she was treated with care and reverence.
This meant that the people were not only concerned with their
immediate homes and ritual monuments: they were also very
aware of the shape and form of the land and the relationship of
the sites to the land. There is evidence of this from a number
of places in Britain and Ireland. The twin peaks of two hills at
Kerry in Ireland were known as the Paps of Anu, i.e the breasts
of the Earth Goddess Anu, and other sites also seem aligned to
twin hills in this way. In Scotland on Lewis in the Outer
Hebrides the Callanish stone circle faces hills that are known as
"The Sleeping Beauty", and at the major lunar standstill (every
18.6 years) the moon just touches the tops of the hills, outlining
the naked body of the Earth Mother herself. It has also been
suggested[1] that the landscape around Silbury Hill in Wiltshire is
a geophysical representation of the body of the Earth Mother.

In Cornwall something similar is apparent at the Merry Maidens stone circle which is positioned so that the twin hills of Chapel Carn Brea and Bartinney are highlighted to the north-west. Both these hills are famed 'holy hill' sites. Chapel Carn Brea has a Bronze Age entrance grave near its summit and formerly a chapel was built there, chapels and churches often being constructed on earlier pagan sites. Bartinney is the "hill of fire" where midsummer bonfires were lit, an act of sympathetic magic designed to encourage the sun to continue shining during the waning months of the year. Something similar may also be apparent at other stone circles, such as the Nine Maidens near Wendron, which faces twin hills of Carn Brea and Carnmenellis.

The relationship between the sun and the earth is a deeply symbiotic one. At this distance in time we cannot be sure exactly how our ancestors viewed that relationship. Nevertheless it is significant that at megalithic tomb sites like Gavrinis in Brittany, Maes Howe on Orkney and the Boyne Valley in Ireland, the entrances to the burial chambers are aligned so that the sun enters only on a specific day of the year, such as the winter solstice, when the sun is reborn from the earth. The most famous of these alignments is at Newgrange in Ireland where the first

23

rays of the sun enter the closed chamber on midwinter solstice morning to illuminate a spiral carving at the end of the tomb that has been interpreted as a representation of the Earth Mother. In Cornwall there is a kind of 'mini–Newgrange' at Bosiliack Barrow, whose entrance is likewise aligned to the widwinter sunrise. There is some evidence[2] that to many ancient peoples the solar orb was a sun–goddess, who withdraws into a chamber or cave at solstice time and has to be lured out again by elaborate ritual and bonfires. Some 2000 or so years later the word "sun" was still a feminine noun, as in the Irish and Scots Gaelic where it is "grian/greine" (f), or "tethin" (f). So the alignment of many of the sites may have been for the purpose of protecting or purifying the megalith with the power of the Goddess' beams. Whether or not the sun was viewed as a goddess or a god, its relationship to the earth was clearly a profoundly important one.

Some key alignments of sites were marked by special stones, either natural or deliberately placed. Standing stones – or to give them their Cornish name, menhirs – are dotted over the landscape like acupuncture needles on the body of the earth. They seem to be placed deliberately in straight lines, a trail across the country as old as the stones themselves, which date from about 3000 BCE, a living trail perhaps not dissimilar to that followed by the aboriginal Australians as they walk their 'dream-paths', communing with the spirit of the earth. The menhirs may have been the markstones of these sacred paths, and some also seem to be deliberately shaped so as to reflect the contours of the body of Mother Earth herself, as in the Zennor stone row in West Penwith, or Siblyback menhir on Bodmin Moor.

Others seem to be aligned to significant astronomical events, such as the Gûn Rith menhir, which points to the Merry Maidens stone circle in the direction of the setting of the Pleides star system at the time of the Celtic festival of Beltane. The Pleides, also known as the Seven Sisters, are in the myths of many ancient civilisations. Another example is the standing stone (now removed), high on Nine Maidens Downs, which marked the midsummer sunset when viewed from Boskednan stone circle. If this was a common occurence, and increasing evidence shows it to be so, then standing stones were features of overwhelming ritual significance that probably included the observation of astronomical events as part of a pattern of earth and cosmic magic, sacred sites to connect with the spirit of the Goddess.

Zennor stone row   Siblyback menhir

MAIDENS OF THE MOON

Most stone circles in West Cornwall were known as the Merry Maidens or Nine Maidens (for example, Boskednan, Boscawen-un and Tregeseal), the latter name of which may be a folk memory of the original use of the stones. Nine as a number in a ritual context is first seen as far back as the Upper Paleolithic area (c10,000 BCE) on a cave painting at Cogus in Spain which pictures nine women dancing in a circle. Nine was certainly a sacred number for the Celts, 3 times 3, the triple Goddess of maiden, mother and crone, and its use may well date back to a much earlier period when the circles were constructed. As it is also the number of months for a pregnancy, this would have been a meaningful number for a coven of priestesses who celebrated in the circles the fecundity of the Earth Mother.

There are examples from other parts of the Celtic world of the significance of 9. In Brittany, the Ile de Seine which lies off the Ponte du Raz, the Breton equivalent of Land's End, was only converted from paganism as late as the 17th century C.E. Here in earlier times there was allegedly a coven of nine Druid Priestesses who possessed supernatural powers, including the raising of storms at sea by their incantations, changing into animals (shape-shifting), curing incurable diseases, and fortelling the future. Even in recent times, their spirits were said to be

25

seen by fishermen embarking on mysterious boats in order to take part in the groac'hed or witches sabbat. And in Wales there is a confrontation recorded in the 6th Century Life of St Samson between the Christian saint and an old sorceress who had eight sisters living in a remote wood, making another coven of nine. It has been suggested[3] that this may be evidence of a cult even more ancient than the male-dominated religion of the Druids, a survival of the earliest worship of the Mother Goddess, driven into remote places by Druidism and still served by a few hereditary priestesses. So in this context, the naming of the Cornish stone circles as "nine maidens" may be very significant, and an indication that they were used by covens of 9 priestesses

The number of stones in the circles is also significant. Most circles in West Penwith have 19 stones, and although the number at circles like Tregeseal has varied over the years between 10 and 20, the balance of probability is that there would originally have been 19, the same as Boscawen-un and the Merry Maidens. Nineteen would have been an important number for a people who celebrated the path of the moon through the great lunar cycle. The moon takes 18.6 years, or 19 to the nearest whole number, to return to her original place in the sky every month, and this 18.6 year period was known to the circle builders and celebrated at the maximum and minimum summer moonrise and moonset. This may even have recorded as a line of 4 holed stones near to the Merry Maidens, which are on an azmuth close to the midwinter moonrise at its most northerly extreme, which happens once every 18.6 years. If so, this would be an amazing megalithic calendar used for observing and celebrating the Goddess.

The circles thus may have been places for priestesses of the moon Goddess to celebrate. One such moon Goddess was Arianrhod, Celtic Goddess of the full moon and inspiration, whose name means 'silver wheel', possibly an image of the wheel of the lunar year. Her wheel was made by three Druidesses, that magic number again. Interestingly, she dwelt on an island off the Welsh coast with her attendant priestesses, a similar legend to that of Brighid, a Celtic Goddess found particularly in Ireland and Scotland, whose shrine at Kildare was guarded by 19 priestesses (later nuns) who kept a sacred flame burning in her honour. No men were permitted to enter the inner sanctum, and she is still remembered today as St. Bride and worshipped by women in the Catholic church. The 19 priestesses take us full circle back to the 19 stones of the circles in West Penwith.

The folklore associated with the stone circles is also significant in this context. Many circles have legends that the stones are maidens who were petrified into their present shapes. This legend is most well-known at the Merry Maidens stone circle near Lamorna in West Penwith, whose Cornish name is Dans Maen, meaning "dancing stones". The 19 stones are supposed to be maidens who danced on the Sabbath and were turned to stone along with the Pipers and the Blind Fiddler standing stones nearby. The legend also was attached to the Boscawen-un and Tregeseal stone circles in West Penwith, the Trippet Stones on Bodmin Moor, and the Nine Maidens stone row near St. Columb. This seems likely to be a relatively late (pre-17th century) Christianisation of an earlier pagan legend referring to the maidens, or priestesses, who danced around the stones.

In the case of the Merry Maidens, the legend is given a double confirmation by a similar legend applying to the nearby Boleigh fogou, where, in the Duffy and the Devil story, a coven of witches is observed holding their sabbat in the fogou. The witches had assumed the form of a hare, an animal that was traditionally sacred to the moon goddess, and ran into the fogou. Both legends, the Merry Maidens and the witches in the fogou, seem to be variants of the same tradition and to point to a common origin: that of a group of women who were originally priestesses of a cult connecting with the Goddess of the Moon and who worshipped at both the stone circle and in the nearby fogou. It also seems likely that, from the similar legend attached to other stone circles, that this was a widespread practice throughout the stone circles of West Penwith and elsewhere.

The legend of "dancing" maidens is also part of the picture. Dancing was an important part of ritual activity, as is evidenced even today in the very pagan Obby Oss festival on May Day in Padstow (see Chapter 7 for more details). There is some archaeological evidence that dancing was performed at stone circles in the late Neolithic and early Bronze Ages[4], and together with drumming, chanting and the ingestion of narcotic herbs, would all have been tools to allow the shamans and shamankas to enter trance states in order to commune with the guardian spirits of the sites and the dead ancestors. There are legends of dancing at Carn Gluze (Ballowall Barrow) near St. Just where in 1885 miners returning from their work at night were reported to have seen lights burning and rings of fairies dancing on and around it. Fairies are probably a folkloric interpretation of the megalithic peoples themselves, so the "sighting" may be an ancestral memory of the ritual activity undertaken at the site. In Cornwall old people used to say that the piskies or fairies were apparitions of the dead[5] and this too may be a part of such memory. The Cornish piskies, like the Welsh elves, the Scottish brownies, and the Breton corrigan were much given to dancing at night, and to leading travellers astray.

Many of these sites have such legends associated with them which are indicative of ancient ritual activity. The Nine Maidens stone circle at Boskednan was formerly the site of a market, which Ithel Colquhoun suggested[6] was a folk memory stretching back to Neolithic times of an association with a sun-festival. At the nearby Men-an-Tol, a guardian fairy or pisky is supposed to be in residence, and this stone also has legends indicative of ritual ceremony. To cure crick (backache) or rickets children had to be passed 3 or 9 times through the hole widdershins (against the sun). The same legend pertains to many of the wells [see Chapter 4]. At Chapel Euny on the first 3 Wednesdays in May children were dunked 3 times widdershins and then passed round 3 times on the grass. Triple three again! Once again we return to the magic numbers of 3 and 9, the nine maidens of the moon.

All the elements of 9, 19, moon, maidens (priestesses) and dancing combine together in the folklore and history of these sites to lead us straight back through the mists of time to when the Neolithic community celebrated the creative power of the Goddess in festivals, when the spirit of the Cosmic Deity was alive in the stones and flowed through the sacred land where her presence was honoured.

WISDOM OF THE ANCIENTS

The interaction of sun, moon and living earth is the matrix upon which the ancient sites were built and the attendant ritual mythology devised. This ritual mythology was based on the concept of the triple aspects of the Goddess, maiden, mother and crone, that was manifested in the birth, fulfillment, decay, death and then rebirth of both the Earth and wo/mankind. The third aspect, the crone or hag, was much to be revered. On the one hand she could bring death and disintegration, as deified by the Calleach, ancient primal Goddess. But on the other she could bring knowledge and wisdom, as does Cerridwen with her magic cauldron. In an age when the average life expectancy was something like 35 years, the older men and women of the tribe must have been particularly respected, as only they possessed the knowledge and experience that would avoid the problems and pitfalls of everyday living. And beyond them there were the ancestors, the spirits of the dead who still watched over the living tribe and who could be contacted through the shamans and shamankas in their trance states.

The dwelling places of the spirits of the ancestors are likely to have been the cromlechs or dolmens found all over Cornwall, but particularly in West Penwith. These may be some of the earliest chambered tombs in Britain (from about 4000 BCE onwards), and as such are likely to represent the earliest religious practices of the tribe. At their simplest they are no more than a closed box with a capstone, such as Chûn and Mulfra Quoits in West Penwith. Some may have two portal stones marking an entrance, such as Zennor Quoit in West Penwith and Trethevey Quoit near Bodmin Moor. Great effort was expended on bulding them, more so even than on the dwellings. The capstone of Zennor Quoit alone is a massive 18x9ft and weighs some $9\frac{1}{2}$ tons. More than 100 people would have been needed to erect it. Clearly such quoits were impressive and special places for those who built them.

Chûn Quoit at winter solstice sunset

Evidently they were not simply burial places for the dead as there is little evidence of systematic burial within. In some, particularly the closed sites like Chûn, there have been no remains found at all; others, like West Lanyon, have yielded large deposits of bones, but research elsewhere shows that often these bones do not belong to one individual but come from various bodies deposited at different times. It therefore seems more than likely that tombs were not intended merely as repositories for the dead, but rather were built as dwellings in which the spirits of the dead would continue to live for a long time. It was to these dolmens that the elders of the tribe would come to commune with the spirits of the ancestors. Some sites have antechambers (portal stones) where the sacred area would have been used for the rituals connecting the living with the dead. Fires were probably lit here for cremation purposes prior to the planting of sacred bones into the chambers. The dead would be honoured regularly, particularly at significant times of the year, by giving offerings to the tombs, and by the mingling of the spirits of the living with the dead. The wisom of the ancients, both living and dead, were an aspect of the Crone.

That their ancestors were very important to our ancestors is evidenced by an excavation at Trethellan Farm near Newquay, where it was found that the site was used originally as a Bronze Age settlement before being abandoned for some 900 years. It was then re-used in the Iron Age as a ritual burial ground, precisely because it was the site of the ancestors. This may simply have been an awareness of the spiritual qualities of the place, but it may have been more: a deep-rooted sense of the continuity of death and life. The spirits of the past continued to be a powerful presence to the later Iron Age peoples who would have contacted those spirits in order to ensure the well-being and prosperity of the tribe.

MOTHER OF THE EARTH

In the Iron Age the main type of ritual monuments became the fogous, a particular kind of Cornish site. Unlike perhaps the souterrains of Ireland and Scotland. the fogous of Cornwall are underground chambers that were primarily ritual in significance. Of all the different kinds of sites in Cornwall, perhaps fogous are the most special. They are always associated with settlements, but are thought to be earlier in date than the settlements themselves, showing that they were important enough to be incorporated into them. They are (usually) curved underground passageways with a narrow side passage known as a creep sloping towards the surface, which was probably the original entrance. Entering them is like going into "a dark dank cave of pulsating energies where unexpected things can occur."[7]

People, especially women, often seem to have psychic or altered state experiences in fogous today, and it must have been even more so at the time when the tribe shared the same awareness of their power. They may have been used as important places where individuals went at 'turning points' during their existence, for example, conception, birth, menstruation, initiation, pair bonding, sickness or death:[7] in this respect the inner chambers at some of the fogous, such as at Boleigh, Halligye and Pendeen, could be significant. Or they could have been places where the shamans or shamankas could contact the spirit world through prolonged states of trance, where visions and dreams could be more easily experienced. The fact that people continue today to have visionary experiences in them seems to confirm this, as does the folklore associated with them which connects them to the underworld and spirits of the dead.

Pendeen fogou

A notable example of this is Pendeen fogou, which has a very vivid legend attached to it. A woman in white appears with a red rose in her mouth at the entrance on Christmas morning. She comes from Ireland and portends death to anyone who sees her. This legend contains some very interesting elements. The woman could well be a folk memory of the Earth Goddess worshipped at the site, the red rose representing her menstruating or fertility aspect. She comes from Ireland, indicating a direct link between the Cornish and Irish prehistoric peoples who shared the same knowledge of the goddesses and gods. And she appears on Christmas morning, the time of the winter solstice and the rebirth of the sun god(dess). That she portends death to anyone who views her may be the same kind of Christian gloss as at the Merry Maidens, warning people to keep away from the pagan site.

Finally, fogous could have been symbolic ritual passages where ceremonies would have been performed connecting the womb of the Earth Mother with the sun god or goddess, who poured her fertility out onto the earth. The orientation of most of the entrances of the fogous to the rising or setting midsummer sun seems to be corroboration of this. Whatever the precise truth of the matter, it does seem that they were powerful spiritual, psychic and ritual places, and continue to remain so today, some two and a half thousand years later. The reason for this may be connected to the very high radiation levels, often double that of exterior background which is very high in Cornwall anyway.[8] Such a radioactive environment may have been condusive to psychic phenomena and trance experiences in contact with the body of Mother Earth.

One fogou, Boleigh, has an indistinct carving on the left-hand entrance stone of the upper half of a figure carrying a stave or spear in one hand and a lozenge or possible serpent's head in the other. Interestingly, lozenges have been found elsewhere, representing the fertile Mother Goddess, and lozenges with dots, as this one appears to be, could have been conceived of as the Mother's womb, and the seeds of the souls of the dead, a very appropriate motif for the fogou.

The Mother was seen everywhere in the land: she was the body of the land. Her annual cycles of birth, growth and decay sustained and nourished the tribe, and her benificence was celebrated by the people in rituals connecting her with the sun and the cosmic round. Places that were seen as entrances into her womb, such as fogous and wells, were especially revered, particularly as she appeared to grant spiritual and psychic communion with her people in these places. The Goddess was alive in the earth because she was cared for and respected, and because people were in balance and harmony with her.

BIBLIOGRAPHY

1. "Silbury Treasure" – Michael Dames [Thames & Hudson 1976]
2. "Eclipse of the Sun" – Janet McCrickard (p96-97) [Gothic Image 1991]
3. "Brittany and the Bretons" – Keith Spence [Gollancz 1978]
4. "Rites of the Gods" – Aubrey Burl (p164) [Dent 1981]
5. "The Fairy Faith in Celtic Countries" – Evans Wenz (p179) [CUP 1911]
6. "The Living Stones" – Ithell Colquhoun [Peter Owen 1957]
7. '"Meyn Mamvro" No. 9 – fogous feature.
8. "Places of Power" – Paul Devereux [Blandford 1990]

It was not only the sacred sites built by our ancestors that were the focus of their Goddess celebration, but other special places in the land were also thought of as being imbued with her spirit. This idea of the 'genus loci', that is, the spirit of place, was a very important way for humankind to connect with her essence, a kind of interface between the mundane world and the world of spirit. It is to some of these places that legends of sacredness or otherworldliness have become attached, and in Cornwall many can still be visited today, some quite famous, others little known outside their immediate area.

If we start in the far west of the land, we find the solid working town of St. Just. A very unmystical place perhaps, but just outside the town there is a large natural boulder called Tom Thumb's Rock, standing by itself in a field. And it is to this place that a curious legend has become attached, which seems to have a certain ring of authenticity. Supposedly at St. Just feast, on or about the 1st of November, which is the old Celtic festival of Samhain, the first stranger into town would be feasted and made to feel like "a king for a day". Then at sunset he would be taken to Tom Thumb Rock and there sacrificed by having his throat cut in a notch in the rock. This legend seems to have been passed down orally through many generations, and was told to me by an old resident, who was unaware of its significance. It is most probably a folk memory of an ancient sacrificial ritual known from other places[1], whereby the king was ritually sacrificed after a year and a day's reign to the Goddess in order to ensure the fertility of the earth. This was the highest honour that could be afforded and was originally a willing sacrifice. Later the sacrifice became a nominal or substitute one, and was almost entirely eliminated with the growth of Christianity, although Margaret Murray[2] has argued that the death of some English kings, such as William Rufus at Lammas in 1100, was a late example of the continuation of the practice [see Chapter 7]. At any rate, if this legend is a genuine one it looks like a unique example of the Goddess–son/consort myth kept alive in a very remote corner of West Cornwall, far removed from outside contact until the 19th century. A corroboratory piece of evidence is that up until earlier in the 20th century it was still the custom for people to perambulate out to the rock after church on Sundays, as though there were some deep folk memory of a processional route there.

St Just has other rather mysterious associations too. Outside the town in the other direction one comes on to the West Penwith Moors at Tregeseal or Truthwall Common, or as it used to be known, 'The Gump'. Here there was formerly a large Neolithic/Bronze Age burial and ceremonial centre, with dwellings, barrows and stone circles covering the area, of which only one stone circle, a few barrows and some holed stones now remain. But dominating the sky–line is Carn Kenidjack. the 'hooting carn' named from its propensity to make eerie noises at night when the wind howls through. Here legends speak of the place of the dead where spirits used to walk at night, and there are several tales of miners seeing spirits and fairy folk from the other world. This is clearly a folk memory of the area as a place where the people buried and communed with the dead ancestors, a sacred ritual act at a time when the veil between the worlds was very thin. Local people have seen visions here of ancient stones not now extant, so the power of the place remains today.

Carn Kenidjack

Nearby are a row of holed stones of unknown function, but presumed to be contemporary with the other sites in the area. Holed stones are known from elsewhere, such as the Stone of Odin on Orkney (now destroyed), and they often had special significance as places where people would come for handfasting, that is, to make or seal a bond between them outside of Christian marriage, which was valid for a year and a day until it was renewed. This may have been the original way of bonding couples before Christianity, and it still continued for those unable or unwilling to wed in a Christian church, or those who wanted a period of being together before being shackled for life.

They were powerful places of emotion and love, and may also have been powerful spiritual places – Alan Bleakley[3] has suggested that women and children may have formed a line along the stones through which they passed a psychic or spiritual 'charge' which had been raised by chanting, trance or meditation.

The area around The Gump marks the beginning of the Tinners Way, a 12 mile track that runs across the West Penwith moors linking together ancient sites from St. Just at one end and St. Ives at the other side of the peninsula. This was probably a very ancient route, taken by the Bronze Age tinners who mined their tin at Kenidjack Castle and exported it from the island in St. Ives Bay. It is significant that most of the sites along the way have special legends or phenomena associated with them, and it is now a unique experience walking in the footsteps of our forebears from all those thousands of years ago. After Tregeseal, the route passes Chûn Quoit where strange light phenomena have been observed dancing along the edge of the Quoit itself.[4] And then the route runs beside the Men-an-Tol, another holed stone associated with healing, divination and the other world. The site was thought to have its own guardian fairy or pisky, the spirit of the site itself, and there is a recorded case[5] in which a changeling (a child supposed to have been swopped for a human baby by piskies) was put through the stone in order to get the real child back.

On the other side of the track is the Men Scryfa standing stone with its inscription to Rialobran (royal raven). The route then goes up on Nine Maidens Downs near Boskednan stone circle with its midsummer solstice sunset alignment, through Bodrifty courtyard house settlement, and along the flanks of Mulfra Hill which is crowned by another Quoit. At the bottom of this hill at Newmill there is a recorded case in 1977 of a couple who were plagued by highly-charged anomalous balls of light.[6] Finally, it makes its way across Lady Downs (where another woman on the walk again saw a vision this time of a stone circle surrounded by hooded figures), and skirts Zennor Quoit before descending to the coast at St. Ives. The whole way has a number of similar sites and happenings associated with it: holed stones, places of the dead ancestors, sacred sites, modern–day light phenomena and visionary trance states. These are unlikely to be all coincidence, and what we are perhaps seeing along this route are powerful places of spiritual significance, highly charged with electromagnetic radiation, used by our Neolithic and Bronze Age ancestors for visionary and trance–work to connect with the spirit of the sites (the Goddess) and the dead ancestors. Such powerfully–charged places are still 'alive' today, experienced by psychically–attuned people in certain circumstances.

At Zennor there are a number of special places in close proximity to each other. The Zennor stone row has already been mentioned (Chapter 2), and nearby is the Giant's Rock, where to perambulate nine times around the rock at midnight would turn you into a witch. There was also a rock in the hamlet of Trewey where all the witches in West Penwith were supposed to congregate, and all these legends presumably contain memories of important meeting places in ancient times, where the pagan priestesses came together at significant times of the moon and seasons

Another nearby hamlet is called Wicca, which may mean "the witchcraft place". And a bench end in Zennor Church has a very ancient carving of a mermaid, the visual depiction of a legend that she enticed a local lad Matthew Trewhella to come away with her to her watery realm, possibly a folk memory of an other–world sea–goddess shape shifter. Along the coast, the hamlet of Morvah may be named after Morverch, meaning "mermaids" or Mor–bedh, meaning "sea–grave", both words probably relating to the original legend.

The Mermaid carved in a Zennor Church bench-end

38

There is also a very interesting field name that occurs at Tregerthen near Zennor. An old field there is called "The Green Man", a very unusual and significant name for a field. For the Green Man was the original pagan god of the wild places from the depths of prehistory, an aspect of the Goddess herself as a fertility symbol of death and rebirth.[7] In many parts of Britain the Green man symbol was remembered and incorporated into church carvings and structure. And although in Cornwall there are very few examples of this, there is one at Mullion in the Lizard where the rood screen has a very small Green Man, disguised, presumably purposefully, along a line of carved fleu–de–lis. So what is this very ancient field name doing in this remote Zennor parish? Could it be associated with the Witch's Rock nearby, the hamlet of Wicca, the stone row and the cromlech, and the mermaid legend? Are they all perhaps faint memories of a time when Zennor was the centre of an ancient Goddess cult. Zennor feels very ancient indeed, and the Penwith moors above almost primeval in their landscape of strangely–sculptured rocks and carns.

From Zennor and St. Ives it is but nine miles or so across the neck of the West Penwith peninsula to St. Michael's Mount, probably the Ictis referred to by ancient writers where tin was also exported. The site has many magical associations, and although it is now dedicated to St. Michael, the Christian dragon–slayer, the vanquisher of pagan serpentine earth energies, he probably only replaced a much earlier pagan deity. The original name for the Mount was 'Din–Sol', which may refer to the sun god Sul(?), but equally likely to the Goddess Sulis, who was also worshipped as Sulis Minerva in Bath and Sillina(?) on the island of Nor–Nor on Scilly (see Chapter 5).

There is an interesting legend associated with the place, concerning the giants Cormoran and his wife Cormelion, who endlessly re–shaped the landscape with a giant hammer, a tale that hints at the ancient geomantic marking of the land. One day the hammer, thrown by a giant from Trencrom Hill, hit Cormelion on the head killing her outright. She was buried beneath Chapel Rock, a solitary greenstone rock, dropped by the giantess herself, which marks the beginning of the causeway to the Mount. Greenstone was considered to be a 'special' rock, and many of the Bronze–Age axe–heads found in Cornwall and elsewhere were made from greenstone. The Mount was formerly connected to the mainland and the area covered by a thick forest, the remnants of which still surface occasionally at low tides. A legendary place!

Further up Cornwall from St. Michael's Mount there is another hilly outcrop, St. Agnes Beacon, that was not 'taken-over' by a sun god but still bears a female dedication. The saint herself is a very interesting character, who also has semi-mythical legendary associations. Pursued by the giant Bolster, she tricks him into his death, by getting him to shed his blood for her into a chasm in the rock that only she knows is bottomless. Again, this legend has very ancient echoes of the sacrifice of the consort-lover for the Goddess of the Earth herself, a legend that has become 'Christianised' into St. Agnes and the Giant Bolster.

Interestingly, cliffs nearby at Portreath contain a whole series of caves, some of which contain red ochre deposits and flowstop. These may have been perceived by ancient peoples as the menstrual blood of Mother Earth, and later as the spilt blood of her sacrificed son-lover.

Other special caves in Cornwall which have always been identified as mysterious places include Ogo-Dour cave near Mullion on the Lizard where the entrance to the cave has a waterfall marking the border between one world and the next. To enter the cave you have to squeeze behind the waterfall itself and look out on it from the dark interior. Places like this, the borderline between two worlds, were particularly significant to the Celts, as were the times between the worlds, such as twilight and the Celtic festivals. They marked the boundary between this world and the Otherworld, and the opportunity to move between one and the other.

Caves near St.Agnes & Ogo-Dour on the Lizard.

As already mentioned (Chapter 1), caves are often associated with the Goddess. At Holywell Bay near Newquay there is an amazing cave that has calcerous deposits stained by minerals coloured white, pink and malachite green. The mineral-rich waters flow over ledges in a cascade of fluid and the cave leads up to a tiny cavern at the top where two people can just crouch foetus-like deep in the dark womb of Mother Earth herself. The fresh waters are washed twice a day by the tides of the ocean as the sea meets the earth in this most magical of places, which was known as a holy well where mothers brought their children to be cured by passing them through the recesses of the innermost cavern (see Chapter 4).

Visions have sometimes been reported at places like this. At a narrow cave below Carn Les Boel near Land's End, accessible at only certain times and tides, a figure was seen walking out of the rock itself. Interestingly, this spot marks the beginning of the so-called "Michael Line" dowsed by Hamish Miller and Paul

Holywell Cave

Broadhurst[8] that links together sacred places through Cornwall and beyond, together with the so-called "Mary Line" which links together other sites such as holy wells and natural rivers, sites that seem to have some specifically tidal, lunar energies. Lines such as these may have been intuitively recognised by ancient peoples as the being the living veins of the Mother Earth, hence their confluence being often marked by a megalithic monument.

Another cave with legendary associations is Merlin's Cave at the base of Tintagel Island, where Merlin was supposed to have snatched the baby boy Arthur from the sea, a story that places Arthur in the mythological mould of the birth of a hero-king from the primal ocean itself. A footprint in the rock on the Island may also have been a ritual centre where the king gained his power from the Goddess of the Land (see Chapter 6).

A few miles away at Bossiney is another more mysterious place of the Goddess. On one side of the road a path winds its way up the valley to St. Nectan's Glen, a primordial place where water comes gushing down a waterfall into a pool beneath. St. Nectan may be a Christianisation of Nechtan, a Celtic water-deity who possessed a sacred well, the source of knowledge. The two sisters of St. Nectan were reputed to live here, and their ghosts have been seen on a number of occasions. On the other side of the road a winding path leads down Rocky Valley to the coast. About half way down there is a carving of two left-handed unicursular mazes on the wall of a rock face, the dates of which could vary from anything from the Bronze Age to a 17th century witch cult. Interestingly, a carving of another maze, the Hollywood Stone, a right-handed unicursular one, which is the mirror-image of the Rocky Valley ones, was found carved on a rock in the Wicklow Hills in Ireland, and now resides in the National Museum in Dublin. There may be a definite link between these two locations of the mazes in two different Celtic lands, indicating perhaps that the very people, who carved the maze in Ireland, carved its twin sisters when they came to Cornwall.

St. Nectan's Glen

Rocky Valley maze

In the nearby Witches Museum in Boscastle there is a further carving of a maze on a slab of blue slate, approximately 18" long. It came from a farm at Michaelstowe, a village 8 miles south of Boscastle, and was given by the daughter of a Manx wise-woman known as Kate the Gull, who had acquired it from a famous Manx witch Nan Wade, who in turn had acquired it from Sarah Quiller on the Isle of Man. Although the stone had been passed down through several generations of wise women on Man, the tradition was that it originally came from "across the water".[9] Such stones were certainly known in Cornwall itself, for in 1958 a Cornish wise-woman told the Museum's owner Cecil Williamson that her mother once had a very similar stone, known as a Troy stone and used for magical practices, particularly to induce a state of mental hypnosis by tracing the design over and over with one's finger, accompanied by rhythmic humming until the desired state was attained. Mazes are a very potent example of a special spirit of place, and they have traditionally been used as passageways into the heart of the meaning of the Goddess, leading the seeker deeper into the mysteries of the self.

Inland from this north coast we come to Lanivet, the sacred centre of Cornwall herself. The name is very interesting: it means the church-site (Lan) at the pagan sacred place (Neved), a clear indication that the site had pre-Christian significance. It later became a Christian holy site, as many pagan places did, and was especially marked as being the half-way spot on the Saints Way, the route of pilgrims across Cornwall from Padstow on the north coast to Fowey on the south, both $13\frac{1}{2}$ miles away. This gives the mid-spot on the north-south axis, and shows that the Saints Way was only building on an earlier pagan migratory route. On the east-west axis it is about 50 miles from Lands End and 40 miles from the Tamar, and as the symbolic centre of Cornwall, it performs the function of the Omphalos (literally "navel"), the sacred centre of a particular area, known in other parts of the world, such as Delphi in Greece, and Mecca. Every Celtic land had its own centre: in Ireland it was the holy hill of Tara; in the Scottish Hebrides it was Iona; in Wales the Prescelly mountains; and on the Isle of Man the earliest Tynwald site of Keeil Abban. Many of these sites were marked by a special pole or stone, and Lanivet is marked by an elaborately-carved cross with a strange figure, located behind the church. The Feast Day was the Thursday before the last Sunday in April, which links it to the old pagan Celtic festival of Beltane [Chapter 7], so this ancient pagan place was clearly the spiritual heart of the Land.

From here it is but a short distance across to Bodmin Moor with its wealth of prehistoric stone circles, stone rows and settlements. The stone circles seem to form a geomantic pattern on the landscape and are aligned to significant solar and lunar events.[11] At one set of circles, the Hurlers, excavation of the centre circle revealed a floor of quartz chippings. Quartz was another mineral sacred to the Goddess, perhaps because of its crystaline and lunar associations. A quartz foundation was discovered at Mên Gurtha standing stone on nearby St. Breock Downs, and the nearby Music Water standing stone is almost pure quartz itself. At Duloe near Looe a whole stone circle of nine stones is made from quartz, and in West Penwith one particular stone in Boscawen-un circle stands out for its white quartz appearance. This stone has been traditionally associated with healing, and in Duloe circle the farmer's cows have been observed go inside the circle specifically to give birth. Quartz was evidently considered a stone of the Goddess for good reasons, and it may be that the piezo-electric charge generated by the quartz crystals were understood as having a special healing or energising function by the peoples who understood their qualities.

At Bodmin Moor we look across towards the border of the Tamar (itself named after a goddess Tamara), and although ancient peoples recognised no county boundaries, they too would have focused on their own special places near to their own tribal settlements within what is now Cornwall. All these places were, and often still are, viewed as windows through which we can see into the spiritual heart of Mother Earth herself, places where the essence of the Goddess was at her strongest, places where a deep connection with the spirits of the sacred earth could be made.

BIBLIOGRAPHY
1. "The Golden Bough" - J.G.Fraser [1890, abridged Macmillan 1978]
2. "The God of the Witches" - Margaret Murray [Sampson Low 1931]
3. "The Merry Maidens" - Alan Bleakley [Ley Hunter 93, 1982]
4. "Places of Power" - Paul Devereux (p155) [Blandford 1990]
5. "The Fairy Faith in Celtic Countries" - Evans Wentz (p179) [CUP 1911]
6. "Strange Happenings in Cornwall" [Meyn Mamvro no.11 p19]
7. "Green Man" - William Anderson [Harper Collins 1990]
8. "The Sun & the Serpent"-Hamish Miller & Paul Broadhurst [Pendragon 1989]
9. "The Riddle of the Mazes" -J & D Saward [Meyn Mamvro 5 p17]
10. "The Quest for the Omphalos" -Bob Trubshaw [Heart of Albion Press 1991]
11. "Earth Mysteries Guide to Bodmin Moor" - Cheryl Straffon [MMamvro 1993]

Half—hidden at the end of secret pathways, stumbled upon near old streams, nestling at the bottom of remote valleys far from modern—day roads and cottages, Cornwall's holy wells are places of healing and contemplation, and refuges from the strains and pressures of 20th century 'civilisation'. They link us back to a more mysterious, more spiritual past, back to the early days of the Celtic saints, and back even before then, for doubtless they were pagan places of veneration long before they became Christianised. The memory of the efficacy of these holy wells endured over the centuries, and they continued to be visited by custom right up until this century.

We may therefore be talking about over 1000 years of use of these wells, and it seems very unlikely that they would have been used so continuously and to such effect if they did not actually 'work'. In a way not really understood by us today, the wells may have been perceived as a direct entrance into the body of Mother Earth, a kind of shamanistic key that unlocked some of the meaning of existence, and the waters understood as being the source of both life and fertility. It seems likely then that the pagan Celtic peoples used the wells for the purposes of healing (making the body whole) and divination (predicting future events) as a means of integrating people with the Goddess, understood as the spirit of the universe that inhabited everything. If all of the Earth's special places, such as seas, rivers, trees and certain stones were thought to contain the spirit of the universe in a pure or concentrated form, then wells would have been a particularly potent manifestation of this.

Later on, the meaning of this would have become more corrupted and less well understood. The Goddess spirit would be interpreted as actual spirits – fairies or piskies that inhabited the wells, and sacred hills and fountains were re-christened after saints, to whom their sanctity was transferred. The meaning and purpose of the wells as holistic places of healing and far-seeing became diminished into quaint customs to do with cures for ailments and wishes for future happiness. Yet, if we look below the surface, it is through these customs that are sometimes dismissed as folksy and superstitious that we can begin to understand the true meaning of the wells.

A dozen or so wells in Cornwall have divination lore associated with them, and many more are renouned for healing. It is as if both aspects were related, the waters being a means of cleansing the impurities of the past, and of giving wholeness of mind and body back to a person in the future. An example of this is at Colan Well near St. Columb where on Palm Sunday (the nearest Sunday to Easter, the old pagan goddess of Eostere) crosses were thrown into the water. If they floated, the diviner would outlive the year, but this was conditional on holding the cross in one hand, leaving the other free for an offering to the priest! The well also became famous as a cure for sore eyes, which seems in some way to be related to the àspect of divining – the one seeing with the outer eyes, and the other with the inner eye.

Madron Well with clouties

Crosses were also floated on the water at Madron Well in West Penwith by maidens in May, particularly on the first three Sundays or Thursdays of the month, linking it directly back to the pagan festival of Beltane which took place at this time. Pins were also thrown into the water, and the number of bubbles rising would indicate the number of years before matrimony. The well itself, reached by a long path between trees bright with the hawthorn blossom in May, is now frequently swamped over, but the nearby Baptistry well–chapel is still a peaceful and accessible place. There are strong healing customs associated with Madron too: a cripple John Trelille in 1640 had a prophetic dream that he would be cured at the well–chapel. He visited the place three times, each time bathing in the water and sleeping, and on the third occasion was cured. Women also used to bring their children to the well on the first three Wednesdays in May to be cured of skin diseases. The child was stripped naked, passed through the water three times widdershins (against the sun), then passed round the well nine times deosil (sun–wise) before being laid to sleep. The ritual (for that in effect is what it was) had to be performed in absolute silence, and before leaving the mother would tear off a piece of clothing from the child and tie it around a nearby tree as a thanksgiving. All this may be a memory of healing rites undertaken at the site from the early beginnings of the well's use, involving the magic number of three, a possible folk memory of the triple aspect of the Goddess.

At Chapel Euny, also in West Penwith, it was also the custom to visit the wells (there are two side-by-side at the end of a little footpath) on the first three Wednesdays in May. Here the future was foretold by sinking a pin or a pebble, and again the number of bubbles gave the answer to any question. It also had a tremendous reputation for healing, and once again the patient would be dipped three times against the sun, and passed around the well three times in the same direction.

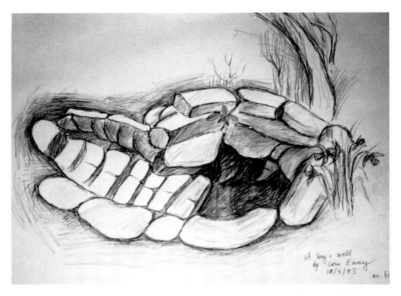

Chapel Euny well drawn by Monica Sjöö

Not far away is Sancreed Well, a deeply evocative and magical site, a "haven of tranquility in the womb of mother earth"[1], which curiously is the one exception with no folk-lore attached to it at all. It is hard to believe that such an elemential place would have been ignored, so perhaps its rites have been supressed over the passage of time. At any rate, it is well used and visited nowadays, so much of its sanctity has returned.

The beautiful Alsia Well

Other wells in West Penwith were also regularly visited. One of the most beautiful is Alsia Well, hidden at the bottom of a hill slope by a stream, tucked into a bank and covered by a small stone structure. This too is a place of immense peace and tranquility, although formerly it was very frequented, especially on the first three Wednesdays in May, by mothers seeking a cure for their children's rickets, and maidens telling the future by dropping pebbles, pins and bramble leaves into the water. At Gulval Well (now destroyed) an enquirer could find out if a friend were alive or not: if alive, the water of the well would bubble, or otherwise become muddy, but if dead remain still. The whereabouts of stolen cattle and lost goods could also be traced by means of its waters. This is extraordinarily specific information, and for a well to possess such oracular powers means it must have gained such a reputation for accuracy over quite a number of years.

Pins were also thrown into the well on St. Michael's Mount, and the one at Roche near St.Austell, the first three Thursdays on and after Holy Thursday being the most appropriate time. Both of these places were holy hilltops: Roche is a rugged outcrop of rock upon which was built a hermitage of an early Celtic saint, and St. Michael's Mount also had an original monastic settlement, as if the sanctity of these places were recognised by the presence of holy water. Both wells also have associations with the sea: St. Michael's Mount is of course surrounded by the ocean. But the well at Roche Rock, although many miles inland from the sea, is supposed to ebb and flow with the tides. This lunar aspect of an inland well is an indication that it dates from very early times, when people were much more sensitive to the cycles of the the moon and the waters at their most efficacious periods.

Another piece of ancient lore was the custom of hanging rags, known as clouties, on trees and bushes beside the wells. These rags would come from garments worn next to a bodily ailment, and as the cloth rotted so the hurt was supposed to disappear. This practice continues to be observed in many other parts of the world[2], and numerous wells in Cornwall, especially Madron, are often festooned with colourful rags, although whether for the same reason is rather doubtful. Wells still attract pilgrims who leave offerings of flowers and stones and are today very peaceful places, although in the past gatherings there would often end in general licentiousness and merrymaking and were thus much frowned on by the established church. However, it is interesting to note that even today Christian baptisms take place at Madron Baptistry Well on Sundays in May, a direct link–back to the Beltane festivals there, though they are doubtless much more solemn affairs today!

These well customs were practised widely up until earlier this century: in fact as late as the 1950s local girls would still go to Madron Well on Sundays in May in order to drop pins into the water for wishes to be granted, unaware that they were continuing a long tradition going back to when the old shrines were focal points for rituals dedicated to the Goddess herself and the spirits who inhabited the place. These rituals later became the quaint customs we know of today, but some of these customs and legends are worth looking at in more detail, as they contain elements of the original meaning of the wells.

The legendary Trewannack Well

For example, at St. Wendronas Well at Trewannack near Helston there is a legend that an attempt to build the Parish Church there failed because crows removed the stones every night. Crows are sacred emblems of the pagan god Bran, and this legend may well point to pre-Christian origins of the well. An interesting tale is also associated with St. Samson's Well at Golant above the river Fowey, which St. Samson founded after subduing a dragon nearby, hinting that the area was strongly pagan, dragons often representing the raw untamed earth energy of pre-Christian times. Another well redolent with pagan origins is St. Nun's Well near Pelynt in the valley of the West Looe river. Here steps lead down a path to a site with the feeling of great mystery and deep tranquility. The well-building is surrounded by oak and thorn trees and contains an ancient bowl into which the water drips. Many strange legends are associated with it, including a guardian elf, a curse on removing the bowl, and piskies that follow anyone who does not leave an offering. Truly a well of elementals.

With some wells it is the position that hints of a pre-Christian significance. At St. Just–in–Roseland, a very pretty and peaceful place, there are two wells, one in the churchyard and the other – the Holy Well itself – just outside above the tranquil creek. It is as if the power of the pagan well was so great that it could not be contained within the churchyard and had to be left outside. A similar situation can be found at Morwenstow in North Cornwall, where there is a pretty little well in the Vicarage garden, but an altogether more wild and lonely one buried in the hillside on the cliffs below looking out over the Atlantic Ocean dedicated to St. Morwenna herself.

With some wells it is their relationship to the sea that is most significant. Roche Rock well with its powerful lunar tides has already been mentioned. And in Chapter 3 in the section on caves there was reference to the Holywell Bay near Newquay. In fact there are two wells here. One, beside a stream in Trevornick Farm Caravan Site, was restored in 1916 and is now covered with ivy and surrounded by ferns and green moss. The other is the one in the cave, the more pagan and powerful, being a natural basin in a sea–cliff cavern at the eastern end of a beach, washed twice a day by the high tide. This is a unique dark chamber in the womb of mother Earth, an awesome primitive place, visited by mothers to heal their children. Finally, on legendary Tintagel Island there are three wells sunk in the rock beyond the ruins of the chapel, one of which forms a pool close to an underground passage. All these wells are linked into the pulsing rhythms of the earth, the sea, and the moon in a celestial harmonisation of primal energy flow.

Some wells have unusual associations. At Mylor there is a well in the churchyard that also contains the tallest cross in Cornwall with pagan sun–symbols carved on it. A very peaceful place overlooking the river, the church still has some strange features. During renovations and cleaning a few years ago some enigmatic sigils were uncovered over the door and on the stone work, probably 16th century masons marks of an occult significance. Another church that lies near St. Ruan's Well in the Lizard at Grade is obviously a pagan site, being miles from any settlement in a round, and has a strange holed stone hidden in the church which may originally have stood on the site itself, the whole area having an atmosphere of deep mystery and isolation.

Some wells were obviously too powerfully pagan and goddess–dedicated to be enclosed or dominated by a Christian edifice. One such is the beautifully–situated well of St. Piran near the Norway Inn at Perranaworthal, the well being enclosed in a grotto cut out of a rock surrounded by foliage. The well is not in Perranwell village itself nor at the church as one might expect, but in fact lies about a mile distant down the hillside, as though its natural setting could not be properly Christianised. This building of the church or well–structure some distance from the natural spring occurs in enough instances to be significant (Madron Well and Baptistry is another example). Some sites seem entirely pagan, like St.Clether's Well in North Cornwall, ½ mile from the church on the side of a river valley under overhanging rocks; Menacuddle Well near St. Austell, an enchanting place under the trees, renowned for healing, divination and good fortune; St. James Well near Chapel Farm at St. Breward which seems to grow out of the very wood itself; and Joans Pitcher Well in the woods of the Trelaske estate which Lane Davis[3] suggested was a survival of pagan nature worship.

Finally, there is a very strange carving at St. Anne's Well in Whitstone Churchyard in North Cornwall. It is supposedly of St. Anna, patron saint of the well, but Anna is only a Christianisation of the primal great Goddess Anu herself. The carving looks like a pre–Christian idol, an effigy of the original spirit of the well in this remote mysterious part of Cornwall. This well leads us right back from the late 20th century to the earliest days of Goddess–devotion in this country. During these long years the wells have been continually visited, and they continue to be visited today, as people are once again drawn to such oases of peace.[4] Some over time have been destroyed or become desecrated, but many still remain, a testimony to the continuing power and attraction of these quiet places. Here people can sit in contemplation, undisturbed by the throng of too many others; here they can touch the ancient moss–covered stones surrounding the wells and connect with a time long past; here they can reach down and scoop up some of the clear cold waters for sipping or splashing on aches and pains. Sometimes there will be flowers left as an offering to the spirits of the well, or rags left in a tree nearby, following the age–old custom. In places like this many have found that the gentle energy of the waters still flows, the harmony of the universal spirit is still manifest, and the Goddess is still alive, looking after her sacred springs as she has done for thousands of years.

BIBLIOGRAPHY
1. "Secret Shrines: in search of the old holy wells of Cornwall" – Paul Broadhurst (p180) [Pendragon 1988]
2. "Ancient and Holy Wells of Cornwall" –Quiller Couch (p133–6) [Clark 1894]
3. "Holy Wells of Cornwall" – A. Lane–Davies (p9) [Old Cornwall 1970]
4. "Pilgrim's Guide to the Holy Wells of Cornwall" – J.Meyrick (p11) [1982]

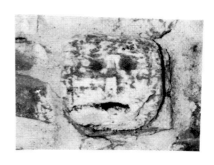

The face of Anu at Whitstone

55

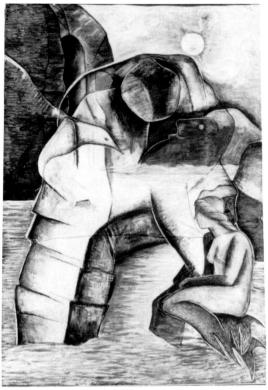

Lying 28 miles off the coast of Lands End, the Isles of Scilly consist of some 54 islands of which only 6 are now inhabited. In prehistoric times the islands, covering an area of approx. 11 x 5 miles, were probably one island, the sea having risen considerably over a period of 5000 years. This has given rise to the legend of Lyonesse, or in Cornish Lethowsow. The land was supposed to occupy the space between the Lands End peninsula and Scilly, which disappeared in a terrible storm, and from which there was only one survivor Trevelyan, who escaped on a white horse to the safety of the mainland: the Trevelyan family crest still contains a symbol of this.

The legend has many similarities with that of Ys, a lost land off the coast of Brittany, which was also inundated. This was caused by Dahut the daughter of King Gradlon, who, at the behest of her lover the Prince (who was the devil in disguise), opened the floodgates and flooded the city. The King only

56

escaped on his horse Morvarc'h, with Dahut clinging on, but he threw her off into the waves where she drowned. This misognyst version of the legend has many basic similarities with the Lyonesse one, the common elements including the drowned land, the one survivor, and escape on a horse able to ride through the sea. There is also a not dissimilar legend set on an island off Wales, another Celtic land, whereby an island off the coast inhabited by Arianhrod and her attendant priestesses was similarly inundated. Putting all these legends together, they seem to point back to one earlier source of an island occupied by a pagan priestess cult, which was destroyed by a flood. The Welsh version may be the earliest; the Breton one has been highly Christianised with the gloss of "the devil", and the Lyonesse one has lost all traces of the priestess. However, a local Scilly legend suggests that several women or 'sisters' arrived on the isles by boat[1]. They had healing abilities and clairvoyance, and warriors and chieftans were taken to these shores to be healed or laid out by the "Sisters". This may be the missing link in the legend, as the Scillies were probably settled in the Bronze Age by people from the Lands End peninsula. These legends therefore may be a memory not only of that settlement but also of the matrifocal nature of the people who settled there.

Some of the best evidence for this is that prehistoric society on the Scillies seems to have been of an egalitarian, settled and peace-loving nature. There is an apparent absence of major ritual monuments inspired by any form of central power or authority[2], and the lack of any such 'hierarchy-betraying' monuments indicates no dominating social or political centre.[3] This is directly in line with Reinne Eisler's definition of Goddess-societies[4]: "What is notable in these Neolithic Goddess-worshipping societies is the absence of lavish 'chieftan' burials...and a striking absence of images of male domination and warfare." Indeed, all the evidence on Scilly points to this co-operative social structure: "There are no signs of anything approaching a hierarchy of places, no basis for inferring centralising tendencies, neither monuments or finds point to an emergence of chieftaincy, and (for that matter) one can detect no trace in Scilly of any internally-generated social hierarchy."[5] Such a society is rare in Britain in the late Neolithic and early Bronze Age, and one that seems to reflect not a hierarchy of ruler and ruled, overlords and ordinary people, but rather a social order in which women and men, and one family group and another, worked together in equal partnership for the common good.

Bants Carn on Hallingey Down

This was expressed particularly in the building of the many chambered cairns which could not have been merely burial places for the dead. Instead they were places more for connection with the Earth Mother and the worship of the Goddess. "The chambered cairns are sacred spaces; access to their interior... alone permitted a ritual communion with the ancestors."[5] This communion was for the purpose of maintaining the fertility of the soil, and wherever such 'sympathetic magic' takes place in prehistoric societies, almost inevitably it is a Grain Protectress or Goddess who is the focus of all such agricultural rituals to ensure prosperity for the soil and its crops.[6] The sheer number of burial chamber and barrow sites on the islands (many more per acre than for example West Penwith) indicates that the burials cannot just have been for practical purposes. For example Vivienne Russell[7] lists some 48 on St. Agnes, 45 on Gugh, 30 on Samson, 55 on St. Martins, 71 on St. Marys, 80 on Tresco, and a staggering 140 on Bryher, of which 130 alone are on Shapman Head Down. Clearly we are looking at some kind of special ritual site that connected with the Earth Mother.

Most of the remains found from excavations in the Scillies seem to reinforce this interpretation. Domestic animals were kept, cattle were reared, and cereals were cultivated: a considerable number of querns have been found and corn–drying ovens identified on Teän and Halangy Down. All these activities are indicative of a settled, peaceful, non–hierarchal society in which women probably played a leading rôle. Bracelets, beads, a quartz pendant, and a greenstone axe (symbol of the Goddess) have also been found, many in sacred tombs, and may well have been given as offerings to the Goddess herself.

One particular burial on Arthur, part of the Eastern Isle group, is most interesting in this context. During excavation of a large tomb, some bones dating from 2000–1000 BCE were discovered. The archaeologist David Tomalin examined the remains of a femur and deduced that this burial in one of the most impressive graves on Arthur was that of a female, indicating that the society held her in very high regard.[8] She may well have been the clan leader or priestess of that society, and if so this indicates a very matrifocal people.

As well as this circum-stantial evidence, there is other direct evidence that Scilly was a Goddess–celebrating culture. On the small uninhabited island of Nornour a settlement has been found which may have lasted many thousands of years from the earliest settlement of Scilly right up through the Celtic Iron Age into Roman times. It is from this Roman period that the most exciting finds come. These include a collection of clay figurines amongst which were Venus goddesses [right] and mother–nurturing goddesses of a votive nature. These are a truly startling find, and one that indicates that Nornour was a cult site of some importance.

It has also been suggested (by archaeologist Paul Ashbee[9]) that the site may have been purposely situated on the island because of the three prominent peaks or carns of Nornour, which may have been perceived as a representation of the triple aspects of the Goddess as maiden, mother and crone.

An ensemble of many hundreds of bronze brooches [example right] found in the same place is further evidence of a shrine there, a shrine that was perhaps dedicated to a Goddess of the sea, who may have been related to Sulis Minerva (found in Bath and elsewhere), and who as Sillina(?) may have given her name to the Scillies.[10] She may even have been dimly remembered through the ages in the custom, prevelant up until this century, of releasing paper boats on to water on Good Friday. Bowley[11] says that the origin of the custom is unknown, but it may be a votive offering to the goddess of the sea. In Bath she is also associated with a sacred fire, and Nornour may have been a shrine to her that maintained her sacred flame. There may have been a beacon there, or on the neighbouring highspot of St. Martins Downs, and on the cliffs at Lands End opposite, perhaps at Table Maen or Chapel Idne at Sennen, or at Carn Glûze (Ballowall Barrow) near St. Just. There may even have been a chain of these beacons running right up the country through Cornwall and beyond to Bath, linking the two centres of the Goddess together in a powerful symbol of inter-visible light. Certainly it would help to explain why the memory of such a bonfire of lights continued right up until this century, even though the original dedication had been long forgotten.

A ritualistic bonfire was also known about on St. Mary's Island at a place called Maypole, a name suggestive of the fact that the bonfire originally accompanied Beltane (May Day) celebrations there. A local resident Marjorie Bowen of Trenoweth Farm[12] remembers her grandfather going to Maypole on May 1st and there receiving bread and cream, a direct link to other May Day customs still observed in West Penwith and elsewhere up until this century [see Chapter 7]. The site itself is very revealing, being a triangle of grass in the centre where three roads meet (and possibly next to the site of a prehistoric carn or barrow). Crossroads sites like this are often indicative of very ancient, pre–Christian sacred areas, and were dedicated to Hecate, the crone aspect of the Goddess. Unbaptised people continued to be buried at such places well into historical times.

Other stones on Scilly are in other suggestive places. A stone row on Higher Town Beach on St. Martins (one of which stones is grooved and one of which may have cup marks) points to Chapel Downs above to the NE. Here there is a unique object – a 3ft high stone figurine, which may be the top half of a statue–menhir dating it to Celtic times, or even earlier being Neolithic in origin. Similar statue–menhirs, usually of Goddess figures, have been discovered in Southern France, Britanny and on Guernsey. The one on Scilly still has the outline of a face, and now stands overlooking the sea and the other islands. Bearing in mind the suggestion that the beacon of the Goddess Sillina may have been on St. Martins Downs, this figurine may be a representation of the rites of that ritualistic activity there.

Stone head on St. Martin's Downs

61

A Romano–Celtic stone altar, originally found on St. Marys and now in Tresco gardens may be another, later, example. It has a probable carving of a long–shafted votive axe, which may be a symbol of Goddess–worship, similar to those on the centre stone at Boscawen–un stone circle in West Penwith.

Another stone that may have been deliberately worked or shaped is the Long Rock menhir on St Marys. This 8ft stone in a clearing in some pine woods has a face shaped towards the NE and may have been positioned to align with the summer sunrise from Bants Carn nearby which faces the same direction. Paul Ashbee[13] has commented that "the top of the stone, though much weathered, might originally have born a schematic face representation", although it could just as well have represented a vulva. If so this too could be a major ritual site to the Earth Goddess.

Long Rock menhir with its suggestive shape

Another site undoubtedly part of the Goddess cult is St. Warna's Well on St. Agnes. Like other wells in Cornwall and elsewhere [see Chapter 4] this well has legends involving votive offerings of crooked pins. However in addition it was also dedicated to the patron saint of shipwrecks, and in the past offerings were laid in the well to encourage the sea to give up its storm bounty to the islanders. This is probably the memory of a cult celebrated at the well relating to a sea-goddess, perhaps Sillina herself, who was later Christianised into Saint Warna.

Finally, nearby is St. Agnes stone maze, one of the strangest and most enigmatic monuments on the islands. It stands on the south-western shore of St. Agnes, the last inhabited island in Great Britain: between it and the next landfall in America is about 3000 miles of open sea. It is not large, but wide enough to be just walkable, and as Jeff & Deb Saward say: "It is this combination of diminutive scale, and its curious setting in a wild landscape, seemingly on the edge of the world, that gives it an indefinable air of mystery that captures the heart of all that encounter it for the first time."[14]

The mysterious St. Agnes maze

Its provenance is unknown. Supposedly it was built by Amor Clarke, a lighthouse keeper, in 1729, although it has been suggested that Clarke was only rebuilding a previous maze on the spot. Nigel Pennick[15] suggests that the closeness of the labyrinth to the sea and its uniqueness in the British Isles indicates something special, probably an influence from Scandinavia, where there are several hundred similar boulder labyrinths on small islands close to the sea. These were used in fishermen's magic as a means of magically raising the wind, giving protection against the sea, and increasing the catch. If this is the case with the St. Agnes maze, some corroboration may be found in the nearby St. Warna's Well which was dedicated to shipwrecks, and all of this may be linked to the worship of the Goddess of the Sea on the nearby island of Nornour.

Meanwhile, there seems to be an inbuilt tendency on the part of the Islanders or visitors to build mazes. Many others can be seen all over the islands, on St. Martins, Gugh, Bryher and St Marys. There seems to be something rather strange and mysterious about these islands that leads people to undertake journeys into themselves, an indefinable something that Charles Thomas[16] has called "an ancient drowned landscape replete with mystery". Perhaps the mazes are a way into this mystery. Whatever the precise truth of this, it now seems likely that Scilly (or Sillina) was "principally a pilgrimage centre dominated by a native marine Goddess."[17] The islands then were a unique place over many thousands of years, characterised by a votive shrine on Nornour, a ritual beacon site on St. Martins, many sacred tombs throughout the islands including a major female burial on Arthur, and a well and maze on St. Agnes, all of this tended by a harmonious peace-loving Goddess-celebrating people.

Halingey Down settlement overlooking the sea

BIBLIOGRAPHY

1. "The Return of the Goddess" – Lynneth Brampton [Meyn Mamvro 16 p.9]
2. "Exploration of a Drowned Landscape"–Charles Thomas(p106)[Batsford 1985]
3. "Bants Carn" – Paul Ashbee. [Cornish Archaeology 15 p11–26]
4. "The Chalice and the Blade" – Reinne Eisler [Pandora 1993]
5. "Exploration of a Drowned Landscape"–Charles Thomas(p140–1)[Batsford 85]
6. "The Goddess Obscured" – Parela Berger [Hale 1988]
7. "Isles of Scilly Survey" – Vivien Russell [Isles of Scilly Museum 1980]
8. "The Return of the Goddess" – Lynneth Brampton [Meyn Mamvro 16 p9]
9. "Ancient Scilly" – Paul Ashbee (p221) [David & Charles 1974]
10. "Exploration of a Drowned Landscape"–CharlesThomas(p154–9)[Batsford 85]
11. "The Fortunate Isles" – R.F.Bowley. (p140) [Bowley 1990]
12. "Maypoles and Mazes" – Cheryl Straffon [Meyn Mamvro 16 p16)
13. "Ancient Scilly" – Paul Asbee (p151) [David & Charles 1974]
14. "The Riddle of the Mazes" – Jeff & Deb Saward [Meyn Mamvro 5 p17]
15. "Mazes and Labyrinths" – Nigel Pennick (p34) [Hale 1990]
16. "Exploration of a Drowned Landscape"–Charles Thomas(p11)[Batsford 1985]
17. "Exploration of a Drowned Landscape"–Charles Thomas(p172)[Batsford1985]

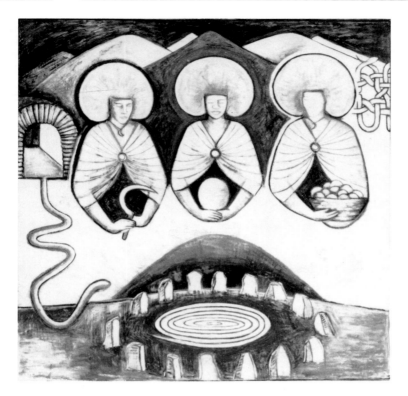

The period of the so-called Dark Ages from about the 3rd-12th centuries C.E is a fascinating time about which we have a few facts and a great deal of legendary material. But even the legendary material can tell us much about how the society was organised and its attitudes to deity. This was not the barbarous time taught about in the past: indeed the society and culture of Cornwall, which the Romans never entered very much anyway, was a kind of Celtic "community-ism" in which people had clearly-defined rights and responsibilities. A semi-mythical ruler of Cornwall from this period, Dunwallo Molmutine, is pictured by Geoffrey of Monmouth as presiding over a democratic law-enforcing society.

The social status of a woman in this society was also quite enlightened: she could rule as a chieftan on her own merits, and she remained mistress of all she brought into a marital partnership. Furthermore succession was matrilinear, through the female line of sister–son, rather than patrilinear, through the male line of father–son.[1] The high status that women could achieve in this society is evidenced by the excavation of a barrow at Trelan Bahow in the Lizard peninsula which produced rich grave goods, including a decorated bronze mirror, brooches, rings and glass beads, indicating the burial of a woman who was perhaps a priestess or even a tribal leader.

The foundation of pagan Celtic society was the sacred quality of the land, personified as the Goddess of the Land, or Sovereignty. "The great heroes, often found with solar and underworld attributes, are her sons; the culture goddesses, who assist, enable and sometimes transform human development, are her daughters."[2] These goddesses were invoked under different names in different places, and were often tribal or territorial in nature, although many had counterparts in other Celtic lands.

The earliest myths clearly show that the primal deities were female goddesses, and Anu is the original mother of the Irish gods, the mother–goddess of the land. The Tuatha Dé or Tuatha de Dannan were said to be descended from her (Danu = children of Anu) and her earth fertility aspect is clearly shown in the name of a twin–peaked hill in Kerry – the Paps (breasts) of Anu [see Chapter 2]. In Cornwall it has been suggested[3] that the strange stone carving at St. Anne's Well at Whitstone could be an effigy of Anu, the spirit of the well itself [see Chapter 4]. Other important goddesses included Brighid or Bride (pronounced Breed), a maiden goddess of poetry, healing and smithcraft, who is also associated with wells, especially at Imbolc, her main festival. There is a well dedicated to her at Landue near Launceston. Interestingly, "Landue" means 'sanctuary', recalling Brighid's sanctuary in Ireland [see Chapter 2], and it may well be that some of the peoples who celebrated her mysteries in Ireland eventually found their way by the trade routes to Cornwall.

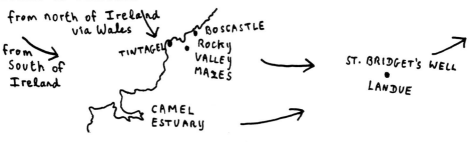

Epona at the Mên-an-Tol   (Monica Sjöö)

Epona, or Rhiannon, were Celtic horse-goddesses, probably identified both as divine protectresses of mortal horses as well as the spiritual essence of the horse itself. They may have given rise to the hobby-horse of later medieval times, who is seen every year at Padstow's May Day celebrations [see Chapter 7]. Cerridwen was a probable mother and moon goddess, possessor of a magic cauldron of nourishment, who also had the ability to shape-shift into other animals and birds, a well-known Celtic symbol. Arianhrod was a goddess of the full moon and inspiration, whose name means 'silver wheel', and who dwelt on an island off the Welsh coast with her attendant priestesses [see Chapter 5], similar to Bride with her attendant priestesses . And Gwennar was specifically a Cornish goddess of love, invoked in an old Cornish legend by a princess who fell in love with the Giant of Treryn Dinas, although this goddess may have arisen as a mediaeval courtly love concept.

Gods included Lugh, the hero–god of craftswork and the Celtic god of the corn, whose festival of Lughnasad was celebrated at Morvah in Cornwall [see Chapter 7], and who in Irish legend was linked to Anu, the Goddess of the Land (the Sovereignty of Ireland); Bel, the Celtic sun–god whose fires were lit on hill–tops in Cornwall; Cernumnos, the stag–horned god associated with a boar, totem animal of the Goddess and the underworld; and Bran the Blessed, the raven or crow god of the sacred head, Celtic seat of the soul. The land of Cornwall is particularly associated with Bran, whose name appears in Caer Bran, the Iron Age hilltop site in West Penwith, St. Breward on Bodmin Moor (from Branwalder = raven lord), and the Men Scryfa standing stone in West Penwith, which is engraved with the lettering RIALOBRANI CUNOVALI FILI, meaning "Royal Raven, son of Cunouallos".

Cornwall itself may have been part of the land of Dumnonia, stretching from Land's End to the Severn, although it has recently been suggested[6] that even in the 6th century it was still an independent and influential kingdom, buffered by Dumnonia. The name "Cornwall" may derive its name from the Cornovii tribe, in which the root *corn = horn, giving a possible meaning of "followers of the cult of a pagan horned god or goddess."[4] Cernumnos had a female Goddess counterpart in Sadv, Celtic deer goddess, a bronze antlered figure which has been discovered in France.[5] All these gods and goddesses are connected to the sanctity of the land, and behind this the imminence of the Goddess of the Land, Sovereignty. Later, she became personified in the Queen or High Priestess of the tribe, or, throughout the Celtic world as Druid or Druidess. With the advent of Christianity in the 4th century C.E, these priestly functions were usurped, assimilated by the new wave of Celtic saints of both sexes.

As Cornwall became Christianised in the 5th & 6th centuries C.E, there were some tensions between the Old and New Faith. There is a report in the 6th century Life of St. Samson, in which the saint comes across some Cornish folk at Trigg worshipping a standing stone at the time of Lughnasad. He admonishes them, but the locals tell him to mind his own business, saying they had a perfect right to follow the practices of their ancestors. And in West Cornwall, the pagan king Teudar opposed the landing of a large band of Irish saints, killing their leader Fingar.

69

Christianity was by no means instantly or universally accepted, and for many years it co-existed with a very active paganism. In the country districts particularly ("pagan" originally meant 'a country dweller') people had followed the old ways for thousands of years, and for Christianity to become established it had to adapt them to the new Christian theology. For example, in 601 Pope Gregory instructed his envoy to Britain not to destroy pagan temples and customs but to incorporate them within the new frame-work. In rural Cornwall aspects of the pagan faith probably lingered on longer, and it only became fully Christianised much later. Even then the old ways never fully died out [see Chapters 7 & 8].

The Irish and Welsh holy men and women who brought Christianity to Cornwall later became the saints, of which it is said that Cornwall has more than are in heaven! Often, many legends became attached to these saints, which seem to hint at a pre-Christian origin, as if the saints' lives have been grafted on to existing pagan material. Many of the saints' feast days are at times on or close to the old Celtic pagan festivals, and must have been attached to existing festivals at those times. Examples include:

Imbolc (St.Ludgvan – Jan 25th, St.Euny – Feb 1st, St.Ives – Feb 3rd); Beltane (Towednack – Apr 25th, St.Teath – May 1st, St.Ewe – May 2nd, St.Buryan – May 13th, Old May Day); Lughnasad (St.Germoe – July 30th, St.Neot – July 31st, Morvah – Aug 1st, St.Sinninus, Sithney – Aug 4th); and Samhain (St.Illogan – Oct 31st, St.Erth – Oct 31st, St.Gwithian – Nov 1st, St.Just – Nov 1st, St.Winnoc – Nov 6th, St.Levan – Nov 8th, St.Melanius, Mullion – Nov 9th).

Among the legendary figures worth noting from this Age of Saints are those who have associations with essential pagan Celtic motifs.[7] Breaca, a sister to Germoe, now patron saint of Breage, was associated with St. Bridgit in Ireland, and St. Bridgit herself was only a Christian adaptation of the pagan goddess Bride. Helena was a companion of Breaca and may have given her name to St. Helen's Chapel on Cape Cornwall near St. Just., which originally had a Chi-Rho inscribed stone, a very early Christian symbol. Piala (or Kiera or Ciara) was a sister of Fingar, killed by King Teudar. She refused the succession to her deceased father's throne, as she had the equal right to do under Celtic law. She gave her name to the cell and holy well at Phillack, which was originally an important pagan centre. Hya or Ia was an Irish virgin (maiden) who was supposed to have come over on a leaf, which links her to vegetation goddesses, and gave her name to St. Ives. Euny or Uny was a brother of Ia and gave his name to a holy well at Chapel Euny near Sancreed, and churches at Redruth and Lelant. His strong association with wells, and the date of his feast (Imbolc) is an indication that he may have originally been a she, a goddess metamorphosised into a saint.

Another sex–change saint may have been Madern, the patron saint of Madron well. Nothing whatsoever is known about 'him', but it has been suggested[8] that he may be a variant of Modron, the mother-goddess of the Welsh Triads. Modron may have been Christianised into the female Welsh saint Madrun, who could then have been brought to Cornwall by the Welsh incomers. In the process, it is possible that the sex of the Celtic mother goddess /saint became masculinised because both the Welsh 'Madrun' and 'the Cornish 'Madern' are etimologically identical.

Madron's Baptistry well

A similar process may have occured with the son of Modron, called Mabon in the Triads, which also has a Cornish form in St.Mabon, one of the twenty–four children of King Broccan, who gave his or her name to St.Mabyn. So just as the Welsh Celtic Triads have Mabon, son of Modron (the Mother–Goddess), Cornish has the fragments of the same tradition in Mabon, who may originally have been son of Madron. A further variation of the Celtic mother–goddesses or Matres may have been Materiana, whose dedication can be found at only two churches in Britain, both in in Cornwall and both close to each other, one at Boscastle (Minster Church) and the other at Tintagel, which dates from this early period. All these names are possible remnants of an ancient mythos of Celtic mother–goddesses, which later became incorporated into saints names.

Another saint who came from Ireland was St.Newlyna who was beheaded, either by her father or a local chieftan she would not marry, as was St. Columb by her pagan lover. Beheading is an archetypal pagan motif that occurs in other legends: Fingar himself is beheaded by Teudar but picks up his head and walks to a nearby village; St. Nectan is beheaded and carries his severed head to a well. This is a specially interesting legend because of the association of the head with the well, as severed heads have been found elsewhere in Celtic wells, dedicatory offerings to the spirit or Goddess of the waters. Originally, the head would have been detached from the body, as being the most sacred part that contained the spirit or soul of the person. Later Christian misinterpretation (perhaps deliberate) turned this into the beheading of the saints by their pagan adverseries.

Stone head found in garden opposite St. Just church

Another pagan image that became Christianised was that of dragons and serpents. Originally they represented earth energies or the untamed force of nature and were an aspect of the Goddess, for many goddesses were associated with them in various roles. (The word "dragon" in Cornish DRUIC is still a feminine noun). Originally the god, king or hero who subdued or even slayed a serpent in such a context was acting with the blessing of the goddess to rebalance energies for the benefit of the people. Later, in Christian interpretation, it became altered to the destruction by the saints of pagan powers. This is why there are so many St. Michael the dragon-slayer sites at previous pagan places in Cornwall, such as St. Michael's Mount, Roughtor on Bodmin Moor, and St. Michael's Chapel on Rames Head, (orientated towards sunrise over the Mewstones rock outcrop nearby on September 29th, St. Michael's Day[9]).

This interpretation is enacted in the legend of St. Petroc who vanquishes and banishes the last dragon from King Teudar's pit of serpents and snakes, used for putting his enemies to death. A similar legend is attached to St. Keyne who turned serpents into stone. However, the legends also tells how, before her birth, rays of light shone from her mother's breasts, a direct rendering of the nurturing Goddess that has slipped through from pre–Christian times.

St. Piran or Kieran vies with St. Petroc as the patron saint of Cornwall. He has pagan associations, meeting his end by falling in a well and drowning, a legend recalling the Celtic dedication of the sacred head to wells. A story involving him refers to the eternal vegetation cycle myth: he demanded the return of a nun stolen from a neighbouring convent one midwinter day and was refused by the chieftan unless a cuckoo crowed the next morning, which of course it did. The nun was St. Buryana who gave her name to the church in the remote heart of West Penwith.

St. Buryan has always had curious associations of a non or anti–Christian nature. The churchyard is oval in design and probably originally a pagan enclosure; the church itself is orientated north of east, the pagan direction, as if it is hedging its bets; the king gave the lands to the Parish in the Middle Ages and Bishops refused to visit where they had no jurisdiction; a Dean and Prebend were arrested, the people involved were excommunicated and the church interdicted; and in 1814 all the carved bench ends woodwork and screen were ripped out and used by farmers for their out–buildings! What remains of the screen shows a curious hunting scene with real and mythological beasts, perhaps a depiction of the pagan wild hunt itself. This was originally the connection of the hunter with spirit of the beast being hunted, a theme that goes back to Paleolithic shaministic times [see Chapter 1], but which became Christianised into the devil hunting for human souls.

Part of St. Buryan rood screen

Even the 18th century sundial outside is composed of astrological signs, and the 5 roads leading away from the church all have Celtic stone crosses enclosing the place. A few miles away is another cross that has given its name to the place Crows–an–Wra, which literally means "the witch's cross". The church itself became notorious in 1975 when Lady Lucy Russell immolated herself in the churchyard in what was taken to be an occult ceremony. St. Buryan still seems to attract the aspect of the Goddess with her catatonic powers.

Not far from St. Buryan church is the church of Sancreed, with its patron saint of St. Credan who was supposed to have accidently killed his father and become a swineherd.

In Celtic mythology pigs were totem animals of the Otherworld, and swineherds often have an initiatory significance representing contact with the Otherworld. St. Cadoc, another Cornish saint, is led by a great white boar to the site of his future monastry. The sow is the dark or challenging aspect of the Goddess, which comes from the time when the moon is hidden for three days every month, and pigs often show the way to the treasures of the underworld, so the association of a swineherd with Sancreed and its deep well is significant.

Sancreed's mysterious well

In the Welsh story 'Culhwch and Olwen' the mythic hero Arthur, elsewhere called "the Boar of Cornwall", pursues the boar Twich Trwyth, representing the great power of the Underworld, from Ireland to Wales and finally into Cornwall where it vanishes into the sea. Here Cornwall is seen as the land of the far west, the last stop on the way to the Underworld itself. This identification is further reinforced in the Mabinogian story of 'Branwen, Daughter of Llyr' in which Bran's men halt on the isle of Grass-holm with Bran's Head. Here they feast for eighty years, without noticing the passage of time, until they open a door on the side facing Cornwall, whereupon they are faced again with all their grief and have to come to terms with it. "Cornwall" thus seems to represent the hidden memory from the unconscious, and, by facing it, the potential healing and regenerative power of the Goddess.

Much later material of the Arthurian romances can be traced back to earlier pagan roots. The Cornwall sisters (daughters of Amlawdd Wledig) of Arthurian romance, whose magical arts weave the fate of Arthur, can be found originally in the family tree of Culhwch as Eigr (Igrayne), Goleuddydd and Custennin's unnamed wife (who may be Anna), and are an aspect of the triple goddesses who weave, spin and cut the thread of life.[10] In the Arthurian romances Igerne herself, as well as being the mother of Arthur, had three daughters, Morgawse, Elaine and Morgan (Le Fay), described in 'Sir Gawain and the Green Knight' as "the fairest and chief of nine enchantresses who dwell on an island of amazing fertility" [For significance of the three daughters, and the nine women on the island see Chapters 2 & 5]. Igerne, as wife of the Cornish duke Gorlois, has indisputable Cornish connections, and may originally have been a Goddess of the Land. She is seduced by Uther Pendragon (which means "head of the serpent") at Tintagel Castle in a Cornish setting, and it is here that Arthur is conceived. Arthur is wedded to Guinevere, who has an Irish counterpart in Finnabair, daughter of Mebd, who was a goddess, and she is also daughter of Sir Leodegrance, who may originally have been Ogyr Vran, another form of the god Bran.[11] So she originally could have been a territorial Goddess to whom the king was ritually married. If so, Arthur was not just a Celtic hero, but originally a pagan god who received his power from the Goddess of the Land. A possible corroboration of this is the existence of the so-called 'King Arthur's footprints', a footprint-shaped carving on a rock face at the Tintagel site, which, Charles Thomas suggests[12], may have been a special sacred place where a ruler or chieftan would have had to stand to establish his right to rule over the land.

Many of the magical Arthurian elements in early Welsh tales point to the origin of Arthur as a sun-god incarnate in a human body. Other pagan gods and goddesses make their appearance in the Arthurian matter, suitably disguised as knights and ladies for the courtly Christian consumption of the Middle Ages. Arthur's ending also hints at this association. Arthur's body is taken to Avalon, an island paradise, perhaps a mythical place of the Underworld, but perhaps also the Scilly Isles, the isles of the blessed [See Chapter 5]. His sword Excalibur (earlier known as Caliban) is thrown into a lake, variously identified with either Dozmary Pool or Loe Bar. Dozmary Pool is a fascinating natural lake on Bodmin Moor, which was inhabited as long ago as the Mesolithic Age some 10,000 years ago. Here in the legend a hand rises out of the water belonging to the Lady of the Lake, catches the sword and pulls it beneath the surface. The whole incident is redolent of the giving of great ceremonial objects to the spirits of rivers in the Bronze/Iron Ages and Celtic times, and links the Arthur mythos to the Great Goddess of the Land.

There are examples of such finds of ritual deposits in Cornwall, such as at Marazion marsh where a hoard of Bronze-Age spears, axes and swords was found; and at Boscence near St. Erth where an Iron-Age ritual shaft was uncovered, which contained votive offerings including a jug and a dish.

Dozmary Pool

There are other Arthurian legends associated specifically with Cornwall. In one of them Arthur marches with nine kings from Tintagel to fight the Danes at the Battle of Vellandruchar. Afterwards they ride west to Gwenver where the Danes are finally seen off, not by the power of Arthur's army, but by a local wise-woman who empties the holy well against the hill and sweeps the church from door to altar, a spell that raises the wind and tide and strands the invasion ships above high water. Again, Arthur receives his power from the Guardian of the Land, the wise-woman performing the function of the Goddess herself.

But it is in another, specifically Cornish, legend[13] from the Arthurian canon that the Goddess makes her presence felt. The story of Tristan and Iseult, written down in 1160 from much earlier sources, is a tale of pagan magic, love and betrayal. Iseult the Fair was daughter of Iseult, Queen of Ireland, and is brought back to Cornwall as bride for King Mark by Tristan, a Celtic prince and nephew of Mark, whom she has healed. On the way Tristan and Iseult drink a magic love potion intended for Mark and fall deeply in love. She escapes Mark's court with Tristan but later returns to Mark when the potion fades. However their love continues even after Tristan leaves Cornwall for Brittany, where he marries another Iseult – of the White Hands. Eventually he is mortally wounded in battle and dies, having been

77

tricked into believing Iseult the Fair will not come to him with her healing potions. When she does arrive and learns of this she herself dies of despair. The two loves are brought back to Cornwall and buried side by side in graves from where a hazel and a honeysuckle plant grow forever entwined.

Iseult is a Goddess figure: a powerful and independent woman in her own right who will not be constrained by the conventions of an arranged marriage. She is the daughter of a Queen, indicating a matrilinear descent in her background, and both Mark and Tristan's position is dependent on the power of her love. She is able to control people and events, as for example when she tricks Mark by getting Tristan, disguised as a beggar, to carry her across the Perilous Ford (which parallels the strategems used by Rhiannon in the Mabinogian), and she is also a natural healer. It is therefore possible that in earlier versions of the tale she was the Goddess of the Land, to whom the King or Prince had to be wedded to gain his power. The significance of Tristan marrying another Iseult when her love is no longer available to him should also not be overlooked in this context. The two Iseults are two aspects – and with Queen Iseult there are three – of the same archetypal figure, the Sovereignty of the Land herself.

Iseult the Fair also has parallels with other independent and rebellious woman against the constraints of patriarchal society, such as the flower–bride Blodeuwedd from the Mabinogian, Blathnait from the Irish myths, Grainna from the Irish cycle of Finn, and Gwenhwyfar (Guinevere) from Welsh and British legend.[14] Caeia March has also suggested[15] that Iseult may be a combination of, on the one hand, a local vegetation goddess whose name has been lost, and on the other hand a Cornish variant of Bridgit/Bride, who may have been known through long years of sea trading with Ireland. Bride may have been brought from Ireland specifically by Irish pottery makers who came to settle in Dumnonia in the 6th and 7th centuries.[16] In the Welsh Triads Tristan is also a powerful swineherd, indicating his link to the Underworld; and his rivalry with Mark over the hand of Iseult places him in the ancient context of the theme of the fight of the Summer and Winter kings over the hand of the Spring maiden, a theme deeply rooted in the British and Celtic mysteries. The legend is full of many such echoes of a time when Iseult was not merely a "fair princess", but a powerful and central Goddess figure in her own right.

BIBLIOGRAPHY
1. "Celtic Inheritence" – Peter Berresford-Ellis [Muller 1985]
2. "Celtic Gods, Celtic Goddesses" – R.J.Stewart (p11) [Blandford 1990]
3. "Secret Shrines" – Paul Broadhurst (p76) [Pendragon 1988]
4. "Celtic Britain" – Charles Thomas (p64) [Thames & Hudson 1986]
5. "Goddesses of the British Museum" – Goddess Guide Group [1988]
6. "Celt and Saxon" – Peter Berresford Ellis (p69 & 73) [Constable 1993]
7. "The Saints of Cornwall" – William John Ferrar [SPCK 1920]
   "The Age of the Saints" – William Copeland Borlase [Pollard 1893]
   "Teudar – a King of Cornwall" – W.H.Pascoe [Dyllansow Truran 1985]
8. "The Ancient British Goddess" – Kathy Jones (p60–1) [Ariadne 1992]
9. "Symbolic Landscapes" – Paul Devereux (p27) [Gothic Image 1992]
10. "Mabon and the Mysteries of Britain" – Caitlin Matthews [Arkana 1987])
11. "The Real Camelot" – John Darrah [Thames & Hudson 1981]
12. "Minor Sites at Tintagel Island" – Charles Thomas [Cornish Studies 16]
13. "Tristan and Iseult in Cornwall" –E.M.R Ditmas [Forrester Roberts 1970]
    "The Cornish Background of the Tristan stories" – O.J.Padel [Camb.1981]
    "The Kingdom of Dumnonia" – Susan Pearce (p152–4) [Lodenek 1978]
14. "Arthur and the Sovereignity of Britain" –Caitlin Matthews[Arkana 1989]
15. "The Search for Isolde" – Caeia March [Meyn Mamvro No.23]
16. "The Search for Bride" – Caeia March & Cheryl Straffon [Meyn Mamvro 21]

Samhain
Winter solstice
Imbolc
Spring equinox
Beltane
Summer solstice
Lughnasad
Autumn equinox

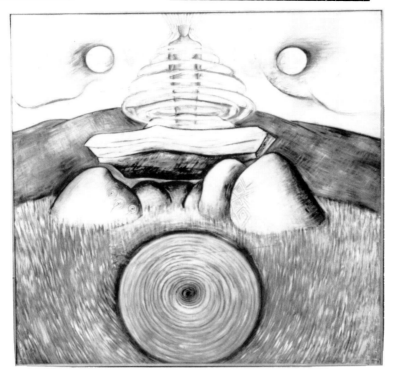

      Long after the rest of England became Christianised, traditional customs that were pagan in origin lingered on in remote areas, particularly the Celtic lands of Scotland, Ireland, Wales and Cornwall. Up until the Industrial Revolution, society was primarily agrarian, and traditions remained particularly in these areas because they were so intimately connected to the season's round that affected every aspect of people's lives. Although people were nominally Christian, in a place like Cornwall there was a bedrock of belief and understanding of the "old ways", and Christianity was probably so readily embraced precisely because of the strong spiritual heritage, and the faith itself which fitted into an ancient pattern of ritual and belief. The Cornish soul remained essentially pagan, connecting as it did to the life-spirit of the land, to the earth as mother and sustainer, and to the regular cycles of birth, death and rebirth. Worship and belief in the spirits (originally the gods and goddesses of the pagan faith) was totally interconnected with the seasons of the year and everyday life.

81

The Celtic year began on the eve of **Samhain** (Nov 1st) now secularised into Halloween. At this time the Goddess began her descent into the Celtic underworld and the land became dormant. It was a time for connecting with the dead ancestors, a time when the worlds of life and death are very close and the border-line could be crossed. It was a season of fairies and witches as well as the dead, and many old Cornish tales tell of the dead and otherworldly beings coming back. Robert Hunt in 1871[1] recounts a tale called 'The Spectre Bridegroom' which takes place on the eve of Samhain, and which features Nancy Trenoweth, the daughter of a woman who believed that "everything in nature was the home of some spirit form". On All-Hallows Eve (Halloween) Nancy and two companions perform a ritual involving the sowing of hemp-seed and the chanting of an incantation, which produces a vision of a coffin, and later the spirit of her dead lover who comes to collect her. All the elements of the old meaning of the festival are contained in this story, which has merely been updated for a 19th century audience. And in St. Just there is the oral legend of a Samhain rite of death, whereby the first stranger in town on Feast Day would be fed and then sacrificed at a nearby rock [See Ch.3].

Halloween/Samhain was also a time for divination and prying into the future. At Allentide (the nearest Saturday to Halloween) it was the custom in St. Just, St. Ives and other villages for older girls to take apples to bed with them, and put them under their pillows to dream of their future husbands. There were other charms as well, including the pouring of lead through the handle of the front door key to see what shape it produced, which would foretell a future husband's trade, and slipping a wedding ring on a piece of cotton held between forefinger and thumb saying "If my husband's name is to be --- - let this ring swing". This probably has links with the old custom of placing two brass pins on the Men-an-Tol holed stone to see which way they would swing to answer any question. All these methods are ways of communing with the spirits of the universe.

The rebirth of the sun took place at the **Winter Solstice,** the shortest day (Dec 21st or 22nd), and the ritual surrounding this day/night was to do with anticipation of that rebirth and the joy and celebration when it occurs. The Goddess gave birth to the child of promise, the new sun–child, and as such it was taken over by Christianity which turned it into the birth of the Son, Jesus Christ from the Virgin, a Christian version of the Goddess aspect. It was the first indication that winter would come to an end and that the animal and plant life on which humanity depended for its existence would flourish anew. So everyone in Cornwall celebrated with the midwinter bonfires, and the burning of the Yule log or mock/block as it was called, usually ignited with a piece of the previous year's log, sometimes with the figure of a man on it, perhaps a folk memory of the Sun God. Until quite recently, Cornish children were allowed to sit up until midnight on Christmas Eve to drink in the mock and sing carols round the flames. There was also a custom, dying out in the 1890s, for children on Christmas Eve to dance around painted lighted candles in a box of sand, a theme that seems to have links with the dancing maidens or 'dans meyn' of the Merry Maidens [see Chapter 2].

Most of our Christmas customs owe their origin to pagan antecedents[2], such as the evergreen plants, symbols of immortality or the continuity of life. The holly was known as the 'witches tree'; the mistletoe was the sacred plant of the Druids and is even now not permitted to be taken into churches; and the ivy was home to the wren who was hunted at Christmas, a folk custom supposed to bring fertility to the fields and good luck to everyone. In the traditional West Country song 'The Cutty Wren', the wren is cooked and eaten in a brass cauldron, a motif that links it to the magical cauldron of Cerridwen, the ancient Celtic mother–goddess, and the wren was considered a sacred bird in Cornwall. The sacrifice of the sacred bird became part of the ritual ceremony of Hunting the Wren which was prevelant in all Celtic lands, especially Ireland and the Isle of Man, and in Cornwall it continued until this century as a general bird–shoot on St. Stephens Day (Dec 26th).

Feasting on special kinds of food at this time is pagan in origin, and over-indulgent eating and drinking was an important symbolic gesture: after the first lean winter months the sun had been reborn and better times were ahead. Perhaps even local festivals like Tom Bawcock's Eve at Mousehole on 23rd December, where stargazey pie is served, are ancient memories of a period of hard times, and the old custom of wassailing (encouraging the apple orchards to bear fruit again in the forthcoming year) is still practised in Bodmin over the Christmas/New Year period. A further remnant of the death and rebirth theme can be found in the Mummers and Guisers plays which used to take place in Cornish villages over the Yuletide period up until the early years of this century. In many of these St. George or King George appears (as he does in the Padstow Obby Oss song), and his presence is an indication of the antiquity of the custom. Bob Stewart believes[3] that he was a Christian replacement of a pagan god, perhaps Bel(inus), "still venerated by the common people". In this process King George, like St Michael [see Chapter 6], was turned from a hero deity who was servant of the Goddess and renewed and protected the land, to the slayer of all forces that threatened the Christian faith, namely the serpentine energies of the female life-force.

In West Penwith the Guisers were known as goose or geese dancers, and the parades through the streets went on from Christmas to Twelfth Night. The participants wore traditional bull masks and carried a wooden horse's head, similar to the hobby-horse of Padstow. The significance of masks is that it hides the identity of the wearer from the forces of evil, and allows a reversal of rôles and conventions to take place, in this case from sober Methodism to anarchic paganism. Dancing to music again finds a parallel with the legend of the Merry Maidens turned to stone. In all these cases Christianity is deliberately trying to protect itself against an older more elemental religion. Another example of this is the game practised at Christmas called Burning the Witch, where the participants tried to sit on a pole and burn with a candle the paper or rag effigy of the witch. [For a full discussion of the witch as wise-woman of the Goddess see Chapter 8]. Finally, it used to be a tradition persisting in rural Cornwall that it was unlucky if the first person to enter the house on New Years morning was a woman - presumably in case she were a spirit or witch!

The next Celtic festival was **Imbolc** (February 1st), later Christianised into Candlemass, the first stirrings in the womb of Mother Earth, the time of the lactation of the ewes and when the cattle were driven up to high pastures. Imbolc represented the growing power of the Goddess and is especially associated with Bridgit or Bride, goddess of smithcraft, healing and poetry [see Chapter 6]. In other Celtic lands, especially Scotland and Ireland, there are customs associated with her at this time, and although there are none specifically in Cornwall, nevertheless her association with wells is still unconsciously acknowledged by their decoration with flowers and ribbons, and in a well specifically dedicated to her [see Chapter 6]. St.Ives Feast takes place at this time and its fertility aspect is emphasised in the custom of people dressing up in Green Man costumes and clothes.

The days from Imbolc onwards are days of increasing light, and this period would have marked the beginning of the end of winter. To our pagan ancestors, it was both a time of concern and a time for celebration; a time of concern because the stores of winter would have been running very low, and a time for celebration because the growing days of spring and summer were approaching. Festivals were held to recognise and acknowledge this, and many of them were carried over into Christianity. The time of austerity and hardship became the Christian period of Lent, and the beginning of the period of celebration became Shrove Tuesday, when the feasting could begin anew. Some festivals in Cornwall held on to memories of this. Nicky Nan Night, also known as Hall or Peasen Monday (because pea soup was made), took place on the Monday before Shrove Tuesday, when youths wandered through the streets creating mischief. It is possible that this may have been the remnants of a very early agrarian festival, dedicated to a grain goddess, which included carrying a burning straw figure through the streets (perhaps Joan the Wad, referred to in an old Padstow rhyme). In Penzance on Shrove Tuesday the people went a-trigging (picking up shellfish on the edge of the tide) which may have been the "last fragments of some broken-down pagan ritual connected with the cult of the Great Mother".[4]

Another ceremony which takes place at this time is the old Cornish game of hurling, which originally was a feature of most villages, but now remains mainly at St. Columb on Shrove Tuesday, with a return game the following Saturday week. The match consists of a challenge between the Town men and the Country Men for the silver ball, an obvious sun symbol, especially as it was originally coated in gold. Passing the golden ball to each other would bring luck, fertility and health[5], and the game is believed to have originated as a pagan festival in honour of the Spring Goddess.

Also on Shrove Tuesday in St. Columb and elsewhere there were egg–shackling competitions. At St. Columb the eggs were hit against each other, end on, until only the victor's egg remained unbroken. All these traditions are variations of rites dedicated to the Goddess of Spring and new beginnings, known in pagan times as Eostre (the dawn goddess). Eostre is assoc- iated with the daily birth of the sun which made her the symbol of re–birth in general, and later, Christ in particular; hence the use of eggs at Easter to symbolise the birth of a new annual cycle. Remnants of this can be seen in the old custom at Polperro where the inhabitants rise very early on Easter Day "to see the sun dance".

Easter, which gets its name from Eostre, is a Christian- isation of the old **Spring Equinox** festival, being calculated by the first full moon occuring on or after March 21st, the date of the Equinox. In addition, this association of Eostre and the moon, which dies and is reborn three days later with each lunar cycle, became incorporated into the Christian concept of Resurrection at Easter. Even the hot cross buns we eat at Easter were originally wheaten cakes which may have repre- sented the moon divided into her four quarters. Easter was – and still is – both a significant solar and lunar festival.

As Spring turns into Summer, the season's round is marked by the Celtic festival of **Beltane** (May 1st), perhaps named after the pagan god Bel(inus), or May Day, "a festival of purely pagan origin, a simple and spontaneous expression of joy at the beginning of true summer."[6] On this day the fertility of the Earth Mother was reaffirmed and celebrated, and this had practical expression in the coming–together of young couples from a village in the woods on the night before May Day. The earliest maypoles were young trees brought in from the woods, and in Cornwall a tall elm was fetched home on April 30th, painted and decorated, and set up in the middle of the village. In Padstow (and in Helston a week later) many of the villagers still stay up and go to collect greenery from the woods to make garlands. This also used to be practised in West Penwith. Hunt says that the locals gathered the 'may', which included the young branches of any tree in blossom with fresh leaf.

It also used to be the custom to hang a piece of furze to a door early in the morning of May Day. At breakfast time the one who did it appeared at the house and demanded a piece of bread and cream with a basin of 'raw–milk'. This presumably has links with the custom, widespread throughout Europe, for the May–ers to go from house to house announcing the arrival of Summer with rhymes, songs or dances, in return for which they were rewarded with gifts of eggs, dried fruit or cake, a gift from the community for those who were the messengers of the season, bringing news of the forthcoming fecundity of the earth.

In Penzance young people sat up until midnight, and then marched round the town with violins and fires, summoning their friends to the Maying. Large tin horns were blown at daybreak by parties of boys who stopped under windows of houses and asked for money, which they used to go to farmhouses and breakfast on bread and clotted cream! At Hayle groups of children decorated with flowers and paper clothes went singing through the streets, and in the evening bonfires were lit in various parts of the town, and houses were lit with candles and torches. It was also the custom commonly throughout Cornwall for youngsters to 'dip' in a bucket of water anyone they met who did not have the protection of a piece of greenery on their clothes. This links with the Obby Oss in Padstow who used to visit a pool near the town, wade in, 'drink', and sprinkle the onlookers with water for good luck.[7]

The dance of the Oss itself is a living fertility myth whose roots are very ancient, and the death and rebirth of the Oss as it is teased throughout the streets is a mythopoeic representation of the death and rebirth of life throughout the seasons. The Oss, a strange black steel-hooped covering which hides a man underneath, may be a form of Epona, the ancient Celtic horse-goddess; nowadays there are two osses, the red (Old Oss) and the blue (Temperance Oss), although probably there was originally only one. They dance through the streets all day but never meet up until they encounter each other around the Maypole in the evening. Padstow feels a very pagan place indeed on May Day, perhaps one of the few living pagan festivals remaining in Europe that has not been Christianised in any way. The music has a primeval hypnotic throbbing heartbeat feel to it as the crowds sing of the unity of all life:

> "Unite and unite and let us all unite.
> For summer is acome unto day,
> And wither we are going we will all unite
> In the merry morning of May."

The Old Oss at Padstow

A week later at Helston, the Furry or Floral dance takes place, a more sedate affair with dancing through the streets and into a large park where the dancers wind into a spiral shape, a serpent dance that was once performed in many places in Cornwall. Helston has also revived the Hal-an-Tow, a mummer's play full of noise, colour and vibrancy, announcing the arrival of Summer.

Another May custom revived in recent years is the Millbrook Flower Festival in a village close to Devon. This has its roots in a combination of Cornish, Nordic and Danish pagan ritual, symbolising the death of winter. The festival, which has some links with the Up Helly Aa ceremony on Shetland, includes the launching of a boat decorated with flowers on the tide at Kingsand to the strains of a haunting "launching song". All these ceremonies show that Cornwall certainly seems to have retained more traces of Beltane than elsewhere in Britain.

The Hal-an-Tow at Helston

The next great pagan festival was the **Summer Solstice** (June 21st/22nd), later Christianised into St. Johns Day (June 24th). This is the great season of the fire festivals, marking the high spot of the sun's reign on earth before it begins the slow descent into winter. In Penzance and elsewhere in West Penwith lines of tar barrels were simultaneously lit in all the streets while at the same time bonfires were kindled on all the carns and hills around Mounts Bay. Fire crackers were lit and flaming torches swung around. William Bottrell[8] described the scene in 1870: "The villagers, linked in circles hand-in-hand, danced round (the bonfires) to preserve themselves against witchcraft, and, when they burnt low, one person here and there detached himself from the rest and leaped through the flames to insure himself from some special evil. The old people counted these fires and drew a presage from them". Robert Hunt[9] also wrote of the divinatory nature of the ceremonies: "A bonfire is formed of furze, ferns and the like. Men and maidens, by locking hands, form a circle and commence a dance to some wild native song. At length, as the dancers become excited, they pull each other from side to side across the fire. If they succeed in treading out the fire without breaking the chain none of the party will die during the year. If however the ring is broken before the fire is extinguished, 'bad luck to the weak hands'".

The midsummer bonfires were lit in a chain from hill-top to hill-top running throughout Cornwall. The custom is still observed by the Old Cornwall Society on St. John's Eve (June 23rd), although it is now heavily Christianised with hymn-singing, Christian blessings and pasties! However, as Cyril Noall says[10]: "(Originally) the fires on Midsummer Eve would have celebrated the splendour of high summer, with the sun at the peak of its power and glory in the heavens, and promising ripeness to the maturing fruits and grains", and this theme is still featured in the celebrations when the Lady of the Flowers casts into the flames a bunch of herbs, bound with different coloured ribbons, representing 'good' and 'bad' influences. With a cry in Cornish:

TAN Y'N CUNYS	I set the pyre
GORRAF DESEMPYNS	At once on fire
RE SPLANNO AN TANSYS	Let flame aspire
DRES LYES PLU!	Over many a parish.

the fire is lit on hilltops throughout Cornwall from Chapel Carn Brea near Lands End to Kit Hill near Callington.

These bonfires would originally have involved sacrifice, a way of returning the things of the earth to the earth to ensure the fertility of the next year's crops. This practice was still remembered as late as 1800 when one Cornish farmer sacrificed his best cow in the flames, and Hunt in 1865 heard of a similar case which had occured only a few years earlier at Portreath. It was the custom of Cornish farmers to carry bunches of burning furze towards their cattle allowing the smoke to pass over the stalls, the walk always being made in the direction of the sun. This ritual may originally have been connected with Bel, the sun god, or else the Phoenician moon goddess Tanit, who may have been brought to Cornwall by the Phoenician tin traders, and whose worship was still carried on there, being celebrated by ritual bonfires on the old pagan festival days.[11]

The original priestesses of the Goddess [see Chapter 2] had become in Christian minds the witches who worshipped the devil [see Chapter 8], as the gods of the old religion became the devils of the new. The old festivals were remembered in the association of the summer solstice with the power of the witches, practitioners of the Old Craft, who were thought to be most potent at this time. All the witches in West Cornwall used to meet at Midsummer Eve at Trewey in Zennor [see Chapter 3] and "around the dying fires renewed their vows to their master, the Devil". This was also remembered at St. Cleer in East Cornwall where since time immemorial there has been an annual ceremony on 23rd June called the Banishing of the Witches, which in past years consisted of crowning a bonfire with a witch's broom and hat, while a sickle with a handle of newly-cut oak was thrown into the flames. Here, the original meaning of the bonfires, as a celebration by the women of the power of the Goddess, has become inverted under Christianity into a burning of the witches. Clearly the power of the witches, originally the handmaidens of the Goddess, were still remembered until very late in Cornwall.

After the summer's festivities, there was a further Celtic festival of **Lughnasad** (Lammas) around August 1st, representing the collecting in of the harvest. This was the festival of the god Lugh, known from Irish sources, who underwent death and rebirth at this time in a sacrificial mating with the Goddess of the Land in her Earth Mother aspect. There is an intriguing piece of evidence from Cornwall of the previous existence of this festival. Until the late 19th century there was a fair in Morvah always on the first Sunday in August, during which a giant figure "Jack the Tinker" appeared, ascended a nearby hill at Bosporthennis and "did there perform some magic rites which were either never known or have been forgotten"[12]. These rites were designed to rid the locality from the oppression of a grim rival, a clear reference to the original Lughnasad motif of Lugh's rivalry with the god Crom Cruach from whom he wrests power. The scene was also enacted each year by guise dancers who incorporated it into a story of how Jack not only defeated his giant rival, but also married his daughter. This took place on the first day of the harvest moon, indicating a lunar origin for the Lughnasad festival. This also shows the extreme age of the festival, as the earlier the date of the festival the more likely that it was linked to the phases of a moon deity.[13]

Although the idea of sacrifice was largely eliminated under Christianity (except for its assimilation into the sacrifice of Jesus Christ) Margaret Murray[14] has argued that the death of some English kings such as William Rufus was a late example of the continuation of the practice. Rufus' death occured while he was hunting at Lammas (Lughnasad) in 1100, and there are certain enigmatic features to his death, including his apparent willingness to go and death by a single arrow. There is also a little-known Cornish connection with the death. An old legend tells how at the hour of his death an apparation of a goat appeared in woods near Bodmin to his friend the Earl of Cornwall, who was also hunting, bringing the news of his killing. The whole incident has an other-worldly, ritualistic aspect to it, and contains elements (such as the date, apparition, goat – symbol of pagan sacrifice, and the hunting by both men at the same time) that hint at a Lughnasad connection.

The idea of the sacrifice of the Corn King (Lugh) to the Goddess was continued at the last of the eight great festivals, the **Autumn Equinox** (Sept 21st/22nd/23rd) which was probably originally celebrated at the end of the harvest-gathering. Here a ritual would take place called The Crying of the Neck, one that has been revived this century by the Old Cornwall Society and can still be witnessed. Originally the reaper who cut the last sheaf of corn – the neck – would run as hard as he could to the farm-house where he would try to enter and kiss the maid. The neck would be hung up and decorated for it was supposed to contain the spirit of the harvest, the Grain Goddess herself, and later became worked into the mysterious figure of the corn-dolly. This custom was also widespread throughout Europe and represents the death of the vegetation goddess ready for her rebirth in Spring in the sprouting of the young corn.

And so the circle was complete, ended but never ended. For death led to rebirth in the eternal cycle of the seasons, and the sacrifice of the Corn God to the Earth Mother was transformed into the spirit of the Corn which went underground and was reborn again at Beltane. The cycle turned and moved round from the short days of Winter to the rebirth of all life in Spring, as the Goddess turned the wheel of the season's round and the people celebrated its turning.

BIBLIOGRAPHY

1. "Popular Romances of the West of England" – Robert Hunt [1871]
2. "Our Pagan Christmas" – R.J.Condon [National Secular Society 1984]
3. "Where is Saint George" – Bob Stewart [Blandford 1988]
4. "Cornwall: The Land of the Gods" – T.F.G.Dexter (p18) [Jordan 1932]
5. "The Silver Ball" – Ivan Rabey [Rabey 1984]
6. "English Custom and Usage" – Christina Hole [Batsford 1950]
7. "Padstow's Obby Oss" – Donald Rawe (p16) [Lodenek 1971]
8. "Hearthside Stories of the West of Cornwall"–William Bottrell [1870-3]
9. "Popular Romances of the West of Cornwall" – Robert Hunt [1871]
10. "Cornish Midsummer Eve Bonfire Celebrations" – Cyril Noall [Federation of Old Cornwall Societies 1963]
11. "The ABC of Witchcraft" – Doreen Valiente (p66) [Hale 1973]
12. "Popular Romances of the West of England" – Robert·Hunt (p72-3) [1871]
13. "The Festival of Lughnasa" – Máire MacNeill (p382) [CUP 1962]
14. "The God of the Witches" – Margaret Murray [Faber 1952]
    "The Divine King in England" – Margaret Murray [Faber 1954]

SAMHAIN FULL MOON
7 nov 1984

The ancient lore, the natural magic that followers of the 'old religion' practised, gradually went underground as Christianity gained a firmer hold. This was particularly true of the ritual formulae and incantations used by the priestesses for the well-being of the people. Their natural successors became the local "wise-women" who retained enough of the knowledge to carry on administering to the needs of the populace. However, with the rise of a male-dominated medical profession in the Middle Ages, these wise-women became a threat to the established order and had to be eliminated. The wise-women were labelled "witches", thought to be in league with the devil (who was a Christianised version of the old pagan horned god Cernumnos), and systematically tortured and burnt alive in the witch-trials throughout Europe. The wonder is perhaps not that this should have been so widespread and violent, but that any of the old lore and natural magic should have survived such a ruthless extermination programme. But survive it did, particularly in remote country districts such as Cornwall.

One of the effects of the witch-trials of the 16th & 17th centuries was to polarise attitudes about these wise-women. On the one hand there was a belief, encouraged by the State, that many of the women – and some men – were evil, anti-Christian devil-worshippers, the "black" witches of so many folk tales and stories, current even up until this day. (Modern authors and film makers can still get away with portraying women like this it seems with impunity). On the other hand though, there was the awareness in the people themselves that there were still "wise-women" living amongst them who had special abilities and knowledge that could help them in their everyday lives. These became known as the "white witches", or in the case of the men "the pellars", and these people were generally respected, if treated with some circumspection and awe.

It is important to realise that both these "black witches" and the "white witches/wise women", about whom we have many details and stories, were only different aspects of the same original Goddess religion. The ambivalence towards that old faith was expressed in the duality of fearing and hating the "evil witches" while at the same time consulting and needing the "white witches". So, in looking at both sorts, we are really looking at the remnants of the old Goddess religion which have become marginalised within a Christian country. We have to strip away the layers of propoganda and misinterpretation that has become attached to both kinds of witches, and to disassociate the whole idea of "black" with "evil", to understand that beneath all the language and social conditioning lies the last surviving fragments of the old Goddess faith.

Amongst the evidence we have for the retention of these old beliefs are their physical remains and the old stories and legends. There have been quite a number of artifacts found in Cornwall relating to 'witchcraft', many of which can still be seen in the Witches Museum in Boscastle. For example, a witch-bottle, found in 1934 in a chimney of a shop in Padstow, contained decayed urine and was sealed with a cork stuck with pins and needles. The urine in a witch-bottle was that of the victim of a witch's curse, who could, through a magical link of sympathy, turn a curse back on itself in this way. The urine of the victim contained a part of the vital spirit of the witch herself, and was a manifestation of the adage that magic runs both ways.

Another find, at present unique, was that of an ordinary wine-bottle discovered in 1952 in a bricked-up cupboard concealed under the stairs of a cottage at Trevone near Padstow. This bottle was filled with a cloudy liquid and fixed to it were wooden models of a cross, a ladder, two spades, two axes, a pair of pincers and two stakes. Local people told the owner that it was a witch-bottle containing the torture instruments of the Passion, a curious intermingling of paganism and Christianity. Another bottle, this time a spirit bottle for keeping in the spirits, was removed from the burnt thatch of the Bush Inn at Morwenstow and now resides in the Witchcraft Museum. A bottle of mercury, used by a wise woman Janie Rowe or Rouse for foretelling the weather, was found in Penzance in 1905, and witch balls, quartz-like stones, were used by wise woman Kathy Collins of Kit Hill. They were rolled down a slope to make use of the spirit force, or thrown when the witch was working in conjunction with her familiar spirit.[1]

Other interesting stones were known as millpreves or adders beads, supposedly secreted by serpents when placed in a fire, but in reality perforated beads made from a blue stone or glass, with a zig-zag yellow line running through. It was believed that those who wore them were safe from being harmed by snakes, or that, if they were bitten or stung, then recovery would be effected by drinking water that had been infused with such a stone. One of these beads, which can be seen in Penlee House Museum in Penzance, was apparently found near Boscawen-un stone circle, but dates from the Celtic period. They were certainly used for many years in Cornwall, and are a direct link with the Old Religion. Other special stones were holed quartz stones, which had always to be in a set of three and one had to be white. [For significance of quartz stones see Chapter 3].

Cornish witches also used bone prickers in making sea magic and wind rituals, and smoothing or stroking stones to ease aches and pains. A 'Fanny Stone' (in the shape of a vagina) was used by Joan Long, a travelling wise–woman to see into the future, work curative spells and find solutions to problems, and two white tusks were similarly used by a sea–witch living in Mevagissy in 1922, one of which she stroked while at the same time chanting a spell–binding song. One tusk was for good things, the other for retaliation and retribution. A "talking tambourine" was owned by Kate (the Gull) Turner, sea–witch of Penryn pre–1949, with which she made all kinds of readings and predictions, by spreading sea shells across a tambourine and drawing her fingers across the underside. Another link with sea magic was the Neptune's Altar, a monster candle flanked by a pair of green glass balls, resorted to by fishermen in need of a good catch, and found in the outhouse of a back garden in Paul. There may be a link here with nearby Newlyn, where the age–old custom of throwing fish into the ocean as a thanks–offering to the sea spirits continued to be observed until quite recently.

Many of these artifacts were, by today's standards, rather nasty, but were used for doing good. 'Get–lost boxes' were used for "passing–on" magic, i.e, to take a disease (such as skin eczema) from someone, put it in the box and deposit it in the middle of a crossroads, a place traditionally sacred to Hecate. One such box belonged to Jane Langdon of Nanpean. A covered bowl owned by a witch living in Ludgvan contained baked and ground grave dust with a disinterred coffin ring nesting on top, but was used to bless people and places to make them prosper and grow. This may go back to the ancient link between the living and the dead, and how the dead can influence the living for good. Witches charm bags often used to contain dead creatures. One belonging to Sarah Noakes of Crewkerne in 1922 contained a dead frog, and this probably relates to the old Cornish custom of wearing a dead toad around the neck as a charm against diseases. One prescription read: "Get a live toad, fasten a string around its throat, and hang it up till the body drops from the head; then tie the string around your own neck, and never take it off, day or night until your 50th birthday."[2] It was also considered to be a lucky omen if a toad came into the house.

97

Cornish witches were supposed to be able to turn into toads as well as hares, and sometimes had toads as their familiars as well as cats. Cat familiars are known to have belonged to Alice Tonkin of Redruth in 1910, and Amy Oliver of Crewkerne in 1941. In a story by William Bottrell[3] Sir Rose Price shot at a hare that ran into a cottage at Kerrow. When they entered they saw an old woman of the house bleeding about her head and face. Beside her on the chimney-stool was her familiar, a big black cat. As late as 1890, there is a recorded case of a hare sacrifice as an offering to the old gods and goddesses. During an addition to a cottage near Falmouth the builders refused to go on until a sacrifice was made to the "outside gods" of a virgin hare trapped by a virgin boy. Some years afterwards, during repairs to the roof, the remains of a rabbit were found in a beautifully-made coffin near the top of the wall.[4] The hare was sacred to the Mother Goddess, who in her capacity of moon-goddess controlled the tides. Hence Cornish fishermen would never mention the name of the hare while at sea or take a hare aboard their vessel. There is also the tale of the hunting of the hare who turned into a coven of witches in the Duffy and the Devil story [see Chapter 2].

Snails were also highly regarded. Until recently Cornish miners, upon meeting a bullhorn snail, would propitiate it by giving it a particle of food or some tallow from their lanthorns. This may be a relic of the pagan reverence of the snail as a spiral symbol or manifestation of the Goddess.[5] In connection with this, figurines of a country woman, a fisherman and a miner in front of a gold-painted snail shell were found secreted on the top side of a big old roof beam in a cottage at Portreath.

Many customs deriving from the Old Religion survived until relatively recent times. In addition to the snail ritual above, farmers would always turn the faces of the cattle attached to the plough deosil (sun-wise) before beginning their work, doubtless an acknowledgement of the power of the sun god(dess) to aid the work. After the fields were sown, if they were not ripening properly then flaming torches would be taken around the edges, once again moving deosil (east to west) to encourage growth. On the other hand, to remove bad influences the direction would be widdershins or anti-clockwise. Those customs around the Men-an-Tol [Chapter 2], the wells [Chapter 4], and the midsummer bonfires [Chapter 7] have already been given. Others involved dairy-women who always stirred the pans of milk to be skimmed, and the clotted cream to be made into butter, from left to right with the sun.

Three and nine are the most common numbers in all these rituals [see Chapters 2 & 4]. Some other examples are:- to cure ringworm encircle the sore three times against the sun; to cure a sore throat pass or carry the person across a stream three times; to cure a stye stroke the afflicted eyelid with gold (colour of the sun) nine times; to cure boils creep nine times against the sun under a bramble or through the Tolvern (holed) stone; and, (a real beauty that combines nine separate rituals of three), to cure whooping-cough pass the patient naked three times over the back and three times under the stomach of a three year old female donkey. Into three spoonfulls of the animal's milk drop three hairs from its stomach and three from its back. Allow the potion to stand for three hours. It should then be drunk in three doses, and the whole procesure should be done on three consecutive days! Finally, a general cure that involves number symbology with sacred stone significance is to collect nine quartz pebbles from a stream, heat them up and drop them in water, taking the resultant mixture for nine consecutive days.

The moon, sacred to the Goddess, also featured in a number of customs and practices. The new moon's appearance was celebrated and acknowledged by going out to see her, holding a piece of silver or a crooked sixpence called a pocket-piece. This observance of showing money to the new moon is probably a vestige of an ancient Goddess rite, and interestingly also involves the number three again in the custom of turning the silver <u>three</u> times towards the person who shows it while making <u>three</u> wishes. Also at the new moon herb yarrow was collected to be placed under a girl's pillow in order to dream about her sweetheart. Garden seeds were sown at the first quarter, herbs for drying were gathered at full moon, rushes were cut at the same time, and winter's fruit picked as well, although timber should be felled at the "bating" or waning moon because the sap would then be down. Warts could be cured by showing them to the moon <u>nine</u> times on <u>three</u> successive nights before the full moon, or by washing the hands in the moon's rays focussed into a dry metal basin.

There were also some interesting beliefs about births and the moon. A child born between old moon and new moon would never live to puberty; when a boy was born on the waning moon the next birth would be a girl; and when a birth took place at the waxing moon the next one would be the same sex. This link between childbirth and the moon actually has a scientific basis relating to women's fertility cycles and must also be a deep-rooted folk memory of the power of the Goddess over childbirth and the cycles of life. This was still recognised in the habit of Cornish women who, after a successful birth, would place the placenta at the foot of a menhir to thank the Goddess for their successful delivery.[6]

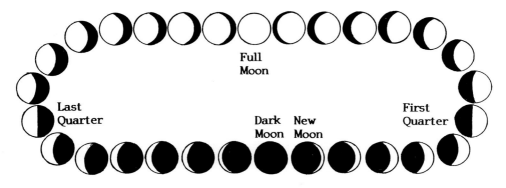

Full
Moon

Last
Quarter

Dark   New
Moon   Moon

First
Quarter

It will be apparent from the preceeding that much ancient Goddess lore was not only still observed but furthermore considered to be "good magic", bringing about a fortunate outcome of events. The ways of the Old Religion had not altogether been turned around and viewed as 'evil' or 'works of the devil'. Two old customs vividly illustrate this. The number thirteen, which in our times has come to be seen as unlucky or a bad omen, was originally a number sacred to the Goddess faith. There are thirteen lunar months in a solar year, thirteen women's menstrual cycles in a calendar year, traditionally thirteen witches in a coven. The 'new' religion Christianity, associating thirteen with paganism, made it an unlucky number, but in Cornwall thirteen was still considered lucky.[7]

Secondly, the symbol of the pentagram has become associated with "black magic" thanks to the works of Dennis Wheatley and others. However it was originally a mystic symbol representing the elements of fire, water, earth, air and spirit, and a protective sigil in early religions. Again, in Cornwall it was still considered in that light, and was cut on doorsills in order to keep evil spirits out of the home. It has also been found (at Conerton near Gwithian) in a probable 12th century C.E inscription on a flat stone with a nine-men's morris board, an ancient ritual game.[8] Even the Christian priests used it. In a tale from Bottrell[9] Paıson Corker and others drew a magic pentagram and sacred triangle within which they placed themselves for safety in order to do "ceremonies" to subjugate restless spirits.

White witches and pellars were often consulted in order to do good spells, and, perhaps more importantly, to counteract the effects of bad spells or "ill-wishing"/"overlooking" that had been placed on someone. For example, in 1844 a group of sick people from Helston were taken to Phillack Church for the enactment of the removal of ill-wishing. An Maggery or Margaret the White Witch of Zennor had charms, salves and cures, and could also put spells on people who ill-wished others. She could make wax images to dispel the 'evil eye'.[10] Jenny Trayer of Pendeen was frequently visited as a white witch, charmer or wise-woman, although Bottrell comments[11] that "there were others who regarded her as a witch of deeper dye". In another account, the "Hag of Treen" was consulted about a bedwitched cow at St.Buryan, and in the story of The Small People's Cow[12], it is said:-

"Mr Pendar sought aid from, and brought to his farm, all the most noted conjurers, pellars, and white witches in the West Country to arrest the run of bad luck that pursued everything belonging to him. They bled his diseased cattle on straw, burned the straw and blood, carried flaming torches of a night around the folds. Fire was also borne – with the sun's course – around sown fields. Bonfires were lit, and his cattle forced through the flames. Other rites were performed according to old usages only known to pellars."

A distinction was made between these white witches and pellars who were consulted for beneficial purposes, and the high magicians called "conjurers" or "astrologers". Matthew Williams of Sennen was one such. One day when he was away (at church!) his housekeeper took one of his books out of the chest, and in reading the words summoned up spirits. Becoming aware of this, he rushed home and was only just in time to save her.[13]

Another such one was the enchanter/magician Pengersec. In the story of the Giants of Towednack[14], which is full of ancient magic lore, he has a metal band with seven precious stones for the planetary signs encircling his head, a mantle and a leather girdle on which were many strange magical figures, and a magic pentagram hanging on his breast. He also had a magic crystal with which he could "draw fire from the sun", and with which he could see into distant lands. He knew spells of binding and could summon up spirits. Against his powers Jack the Tinkard possessed a charm–stone or amulet with which he defeated him. He invoked the spirit of the stone by touching his forehead and mouth with it, used a nine times deosil spell to free Genevra his bride from the enchantment, and blessed the stone with a magic incantation. Finally he "descends to mother earth", and Bottrell comments[15]: "It is certain that the loadstone was regarded here as a kind of divinity, or at least it was venerated as the shrine of a deity". Later[16] he gives some protective spells used by conjurers, pellars and wise women, including the magic square which can be read in any direction:

```
S A T O R
A R E P O
T E N E T
O P E R A
R O T A S
```

He also gives some magic words (NALGAH, TETRAGRAMMATON, etc), a drawing of a bird with eggs (again a Goddess symbol), and a drawing of the planetary signs for the Sun, Jupiter and Venus, followed by a cross, pentagram and other sigils. He suggests that many practitioners of these arts are ignorant of the meaning of the fomulae, but "regard them as powerful words and signs that have been handed down from ancient times".

Witchcraft in its original sense was a living tradition in Cornwall, probably one of the very last places in Great Britain where it was extensively acknowledged and followed. The seventh son of a seventh son, or seventh daughter of a seventh daughter were born with the gift of charming, and made the most noted practitioners of the arts, but anyone might become a witch who touched a logan rock (rocking stone) nine times at midnight. In some areas, witchcraft was so well known that whole villages were associated with it. St. Levan people (near Lands End) used to be known as the 'St. Levan Witches', from the general belief that the inhabitants of this remote parish were in past times "much addicted to the power of witchcraft".

The Logan Rock at St. Levan

Old folks held that in fact all the West Country witches used to meet up at nearby Treen, and, as is usual with these things, their rituals and rites got rather misinterpreted. In the case of the Treen witches they were supposed to be able to travel by means of ragwort stems to other Celtic lands such as Wales and Brittany! They also gathered at Trewey Downs near Zennor on Midsummer Eve where they lit fires on the surrounding cromlechs, which takes us directly back to the midsummer bonfires lit at this time [see Chapter 7].

All this cumulative wealth of reference, detail, custom and lore appertaining to wise women and witches is an indication that in Cornwall the healing and protective powers of the Goddess lingered on until very late indeed. In fact, as the next chapter shows, they never really died out at all.

BIBLIOGRAPHY
1. "Archaeology of Ritual and Magic"–Ralph Merrifield(p180)[Batsford 1987]
2. "Cornish Feasts and Folklore" – Margaret Courtney (p155) [Beare 1890]
3. "Hearthside Stories of West Cornwall" –William Bottrell (III,91) [1873]
4. "The Leaping Hare" – David Thomson (p222) [Faber 1972]
5. "The Goddess of the Stones" –George Terence Meaden(p153)[Souvenir 1991]
6. "West Country Wicca" – Rhiannon Ryall (p54) [Phoenix 1989]
7. "Cornish Feasts and Folklore" – Margaret Courtney (p139) [Beare 1890]
8. "Gwithian" – Charles Thomas [Earle 1964]
9. "Hearthside Stories of West Cornwall" –William Bottrell (I,233) [1870]
10. ibid. (I,79-80, 90)
11. ibid. (II, 154)
12. ibid. (II, 75)
13. ibid. (III, 142)
14. ibid. (I, 1-46)
15. ibid. (I, 41)
16. ibid. (III, 190-1)

Perhaps because Cornwall was a Celtic land, or perhaps because the ancient sites are still (relatively) unspoilt and undeveloped, she has attracted many modern-day pagans, so that there is now a thriving network of people living there and loving the land. Some work as individuals, others belong to groups or covens; some work primarily indoors, others like to feel the wind in their hair and the ground beneath their feet; some belong to specific magical and ritual traditions, others create whatever seems most apt for themselves and their friends. Most know each other and mutually respect each other's approaches and ways of connecting with the spirit of the universe. Some are specifically Goddess-celebrating, or Goddess-orientated, others search for a balance between the goddess and her consort-son, the god in the eternal cycle. Most love and care for the ancient sites, and build their ritual celebrations upon traditional foundations, adapting them for the 20th & 21st centuries.

A number of Goddess–celebrating groups have flourished in West Cornwall for some years now. One particular Group's aim was to give thanks to Mother Earth for her sustinence by celebrating the year's cycle of festivals at the sacred sites. There was no hierarchy of priests and priestesses, but rather a sharing of ideas and energies in which each member was encouraged to develop their own talents and abilities for the Group, the Goddess and themselves. The Group generally attracted those people who instinctively felt the pagan world around and inside themselves, even if they were unable or unwilling to pin a label on it. Its function was to be at one with the Goddess, and to celebrate the turning of the year's cycle in the sacred land of their ancestors, as is shown in the following examples.

Beltane was celebrated with maypole dancing and musicians up on a Carn the evening before, a joyful way to see in the Spring and to reclaim the original meaning of the dance. This tradition continues and is now (1993) in its 5th year.

After a few hours sleep, a hill would be climbed to a wooded ancient site to see in the dawn. There, each would find a favourite tree to commune with the devas or woodland spirits. From the depths of the wood would come the steady heart-beat of a drum, as everyone gradually moved back together to the centre where they met and embraced. The Spring Maiden would be dressed with flowers and ribbons, and she would then lead a dance through the woods, as flutes, tambourines, rattles and bells would be joyfully played, and songs sung:

"In the centre of the wood, cauldron stands and candles burn,
We have danced the dance of summer, the Goddess will return."

One of the trees would then be dressed with greenery and ribbons, and the dawn chorus would accompany the return for breakfast, before many would make their way to Padstow, dancing through the streets all day with the Obby Oss!

The Spring maiden in the woods at Beltane

Summer Solstice would bring another sunrise festival. On a dark early morning of 21st June, fires could be seen on hilltops as groups would gather all over Cornwall to welcome the sun on the longest day. Drums would beat and incantations be made as the sun was chanted up over the horizon: "We are at one with the infinite sun, for ever and ever and ever". Hopes and wishes for the future would be expressed: "The fruits of mother earth have started to ripen, so let us begin to ripen within ourselves those fruits we wish to nurture, and let this time of sunshine and warmth encourage those things to grow that we have planted within us." Good energies for the health of the planet would be sent out, and a simple feast shared together.

Lughnasad was usually celebrated on the moors at an ancient site near to Morvah, with its traditional Lammas feast-day. There in a field the Corn King would be cut down and returned to the earth. John Barleycorn would be fashioned from some sheafs of corn and given as a gift to the Goddess in the sacred site.

John Barleycorn is given to the Goddess
108

Then a landscape maze would be built and one by one, each would walk to its centre and out again, as the others meditated on the passing of summer's gifts. A song of Lughnasad would be sung: "All that we are is an ancient dream, Born on the wheel of the season's green"* and the afternoon would finish with a great feast of summer's fruits and fruit wines on the grass. It was a time of great joy and sharing, tinged with the awareness of the passing of time.

Autumn Equinox was a time when all met to prepare for the going down into the dark. Each person might bring a special stone that had been charged with energy during the summer months, and some corn and fruits from summer's harvest. The corn and fruits would be returned to the earth, and the stones placed around the base of an ancient standing stone to amplify their power. Words would be spoken of the meaning: "Everything lost is found again in a new form. Everything hurt is healed again in a new life. Everything feared is faced again in a new day". Candles would be lit, hands joined in a circle, and the shared energy and love would flow into the stones and be taken away to be a talisman during the winter.

Samhain, traditionally the most magic of times when the spirits of the ancestors were close to the world of the living, would often be celebrated in a fogou. Perhaps a Samhain song would be quietly sung:

'Draw back the veil that is pale in the stars,
Walk with us, spirits unseen.
Lord of the Shadows come weave us your will,
Dark Mother calls from the hill."*

There would be a deep meditation, followed by a low ohming chant building to a climax as the ancient primal Goddess Calleach, or the dark Goddess Hecate, would be invoked. Some people would trace their fingers around maze stones to induce a meditative state, others scry into a bowl of water illuminated by the moon shining down into the fogou entrance. An atmosphere of great mystery and deep inner contemplation. At the end there would be a quiet grounding, in order to hold themselves safe for the changes in their lives.

Winter Solstice would take place at an ancient site under the cold night sky. The Crone would oversee all and set proceedings in motion with the burning of the Yule log which would be re-lit from the previous year's block. Flaming torches would burn bright at the four quarters, and a dedication made to the Earth Mother, about to give birth to the Sun Child. Often a holed stone, or dolmen entrance would be used, and each person would then crawl through to symbolise inner rebirth and the rebirth of the sun. All would then dance around the stones and the lights and the body of Mother Earth herself, dancing · themselves alive, as the music played and the songs were sung:

'Then born from the night of long shadows,
Warm grows the light of the sun,
Strong grows the oak from the holly
As the earthyear turns and wakes the newborn one.'*

Houses would be decorated with holly, ivy and other greenery from the woods around, and celebrations of eating, drinking and giving presents would continue for several days along with the rest of the population!

Imbolc, the festival of the Goddess Bride/Bridgit, was usually celebrated at a holy well and sometimes along the seashore too. A procession would be made with candles in jars along to the well, a faery trail of twinkling lights. The candles would be placed around the well and extinguished for a quiet mediation. Then Bride/Bridgit would be invoked, and her presence usually sensed or felt. One might come forth as her with a crown of candles, holding and shielding a light. This would be passed round and all would light their candles from hers. Each would then go to the well, collect some sacred water, saying private dedications, and then bless each other with the water, finally giving it back to the earth. Candles would burn bright in the crevices around the well, reflected in the deep waters. It would be a time of much magic, as the sacred place was blessed and the gentle power of the Goddess was taken within each person.

'Imbolc, Imbolc – the season of rebirth,
Feel the infant stirring in the waters of the earth.
Imbolc, Imbolc – the light will still return,
Warm the earth this winter's night – let the candles burn.'*

Candles at the well at Imbolc

111

Finally in the ritual cycle of the year, Spring Equinox would be given over to celebrate the festival of Eostre, the Goddess of Spring. She, the dark maiden, would return so that winter could release its hold upon the Earth and let it blossom. Her apperance would be celebrated with spring flowers garlanded into wreaths with ribbons and shells, painted eggs shared and given back into the earth, sacred cakes baked from ingredients supplied by everyone, and seeds planted into the earth with hopes for the future: "Out of winter comes spring, out of death comes life, as the seed that is sown germinates and grows, leafs and blossoms, bears fruit and seed of its own. So mote it always be."

There are other groups throughout Cornwall that have formed, merged, separated and re-grouped over the years. At Harmony Pottery at Scorrier near Redruth three women have organised regular festival celebrations to which all interested people were welcome, and a full account of these has been given in the magazine "Meyn Mamvro" (nos. 19 & 20). These celebrations included bonfires and smudging, spiral and circle dancing, music and musicians, maze walking and meditation, drumming and singing, sharing food and poetry.

Bonfire celebrations at Harmony

Geraldine Andrew, at whose place the celebrations have occured speaks about it in this way:
"My understanding of magic and paganism has evolved experientially. We read many books, and often we are told we need a mediator, priest or priestess between us and the Goddess/God. However we are all spiritual beings, we are all divine, and we must seek the will of nature, using the power of the tides, of the seasons, the strange and changing light of the moon, the blessings of the wind. We all contain the creative force, the power which we must use with love to support our Earth Mother and treat her with care and respect. In our festivals we try to express our deep love of the land, of Cornwall, the indescribable beauty and wonder of creation."[1]

Down in the Lizard there is a more private Group who are the nature mystics and work with the serpentine energies there. They see themselves as inheritors of the shamanic tradition, and guardians of the valleys there. In an article in "Meyn Mamvro", Robin Ellis wrote about them in this way:
"People are naturally attracted to the fissures, sea–caves and wells by the snake–breath, especially at the time of the full moon! They feel a compulsion to go and look in, which seems to have a hypnotic effect on them; smelling its snake–breath smell of rock and water, hearing its sounds, the voices, the magic, the hallucinations – dreaming and feeding on the energies. 'Drowsing here I've heard sounds and seen visions that have given me life!' People have claimed at times to have been benignly possessed by a spirit from within the earth, and this part of Cornwall is full of legends about snakes that have turned themselves into people, to walk abroad in either human or serpent form! However, it is much more likely that people can become the vehicle for a tremendously powerful earth–force, that enables them to heal and do magic."[2]

As well as the more formal coven structure of some Groups, there are many other ways of being and relating. Some people are "hedge witches", working alone with the plants and herbs of the land, celebrating the wheel of life with personal candle magic and inner contemplation; some may come together in twos and threes, perhaps to sing the land alive at ancient sites, or to do healing and psychic growth together. Sometimes people meet up for discussions or storytime evenings, those who are interested in tarot, divination, shaminism, reincarnation, and many other pagan-related topics. From time to time there are workshops on the Goddess within, sacred dance, past–life reincarnation, and other themes. There is much variety of activity, much multiplicity of choice.

Some women prefer to work only or mainly with other women, so there are Women's ritual groups too, who meet at full moons, and sometimes new moons as well. At the new moon the women might meet indoors and share the events of their lives and their feelings about the world. A common theme may emerge, perhaps to do with the concerns of the planet, such as environmental devastation, or the exploitation of indigeneous peoples. It can be more personal as well, to do with relation-ships, health problems, menstruation, or healing out difficult emotions. From this a ritual may be devised to help one or all the Group, the cauldron may be placed in the centre and the women then put into it symbolically those things they wish to be rid of, or take from it those things they need. Some chanting may be done, or slow drumming leading to inner journeying or meditation. At the full moon they may meet at a local stone circle or well and there invoke one of the Goddesses, such as Artemis for independence, or Athena for wisdom, and dance her alive around the stones in love and friendship. The women share their lives, their fears and their hopes for the period of the ritual, and keep the Goddess present in all of them together.

Paganism or Goddess–spirituality in Cornwall is a very loosely–constructed network. There is no single central organisation, no hierarchy of enlightened groups, no fixed dogma or book of rules. Each individual or group of individuals decides for themselves what their needs are and how it best works for them. Its diversity is its strength, its lack of cohesion a relection of a new way of growing. Many feel that if the world is to have any future then humankind must learn again to love and respect the earth as in the past, and therefore these ways should be accessible and approachable by everyone who is genuinely interested. They seek harmony with other ways and approaches, without losing the essential power and magic of the belief, a power and magic that has sustained it through 20,000 years of growth and 2000 years of repression.

The Goddess continues to be celebrated in Cornwall, perhaps more now than for many a long year, in rituals and activities based on traditional practices but adapted to meet the needs of today. The legendary aspects of Celtic lore, together with elements of the meaning of the prehistoric sacred sites, their relationship to the sun and the moon, the earth and her seasons, the elements and the elementals, are set in a ritual context by individuals and groups. They are strands in a network, working separately to re–awaken a new kind of spirituality for a new way of living. But paradoxically it is a spirituality that is as old as time itself, a spirituality that began in the caves of our paleolithic ancestors and continued in one form or another throughout centuries of change and adaptation. The result is a long heritage of ancient wisdom, a well of tradition into which people can still dip to build a powerful matrix of energies focused for meditation, initiation, rebirth, healing and cleansing. Cornwall, a land of great beauty which still lives today, is thus, even after 20,000 or so years, still the Land of the Goddess.

REFERENCES
1. "Harmony Celebrations" – Geraldine Andrew [Meyn Mamvro no.19]
2. "Spirit of the Lizard" – Robin Ellis [Meyn Mamvro no.12]
* Lyrics from "Ancient Dream" cycle of songs for the eight festivals by Michael Woolf & Rachel Garcia (originally written for a pagan group in Cornwall). Available on cassette from Rachel Garcia, 21 Cremorne Road, Chelsea, London, SW10 ONB.

PICTURE CREDITS

MARJORIANNE ROWLAND for artwork on p 9, 10, 55, 73, 80, 114.

MONICA SJÖÖ for artwork on p 11, 22, 34, 46, 49, 56, 66, 68, 81, 94, 105.

CAEIA MARCH for artwork on p 12, 13, 15, 17, 96, 100.

GABRIELLE HAWKES for artwork on p 21.

ROSE LEWIS for artwork on p 40, and photograph on p 41 (left).

SU BAYFIELD for artwork on p 71, 75, 79, 116.

GERALDINE ANDREW for artwork on p 82, 83, 85, 86, 91, 92, and photograph on p 112.

CHERYL STRAFFON for photographs on front cover, p 23, 25, 27, 30, 32, 42, 43, 48, 50, 52, 55, 58, 61, 62, 63, 65, 77, 88, 89, 106, 107, 108, 110, 111.

JENNY CROXFORD for photograph on p 41 (right).

Other artwork on p 18, 36 (lower), 72 from "St Just" – Rev. Buller [1842]; on p 36 (upper), 37, 38, 74, 103 from "A week at the Land's End" – J.T. Blight [1861]; & on p 98 from "Traditions and Hearthside Stories of West Cornwall" – William Bottrell – artwork by J.T.Blight [1870]. Drawing on p 59 by Glen Leon from a find by Ashbee & on p 60 by David Neal from Isles of Scilly Museum Publication on Nornour [reproduced from Meyn Mamvro no.16].

THE ARTISTS

GERALDINE ANDREW lives at Harmony Pottery at Scorrier near Redruth. She is in her 40s, a potter and a sculptor, and also does astrology, massage and painting. She is a Scorpio, and feels that every part of her life is influenced by her spiritual beliefs. She also looks quite fetching in her witches hat when serving tea for the family!

SU BAYFIELD is in her late 30s, lives in West Penwith and has a strong feel for the spirituality of the land there. She is knowledgable about the ancient sites and feels connected to their power. She is an Aquarian who is interested in magic and herbalism for the purposes of healing.

GABRIELLE HAWKES is an artist living in St.Just-in-Penwith, and is known particularly for her screen-prints and paintings. Together with photographer Tom Henderson-Smith she runs Visions and Journeys art gallery, and has a deep relationship with the area and the mysteries of its ancient landscape. She is drawn strongly to the megalithic sites, and painting them is a form of meditation, a way of opening herself up to their subtle energies.

ROSE LEWIS moved from California in 1990 to Cornwall, where the land called strongly to her. She is very interested in Native American, Dzogchen, and Celtic spirituality, which she expresses through art and music, dance and song. She is especially drawn to caves, which to her are the dark spaces in the belly of the earth. She works for an environmental protection group, and is constantly inspired by the energy and spirit of the land.

CAEIA MARCH was born on the Isle of Man, and her ancestors on her mother's side were Manx Celts. She has lived in West Penwith since 1988, loves the land, sea and sky there, and is a keen gardener. She is the author of three lesbian novels published by The Womens Press: "Three Ply Yarn"; "The Hide and Seek Files"; and "Fire! Fire!". The last two and her new novel "Reflections" (work in progress) are set partly in Cornwall.

MARJORIANNE ROWLAND has lived in Cornwall for 15 years, is aged 46, and runs courses and workshops on holistic Aroma Therapy. She is a healer, counsellor and illustrator, and an ordained Priestess of Sophia in the Fellowship of Isis. She celebrates the innate beauty of the female body using bodywork, movement and dance. She is also an enthusiastic member of the Middle Eastern Dancing Association (U.K).

MONICA SJÖÖ is a visionary artist who also writes. She has spent many years working in and with the women's movement in all its aspects. She is an initiator of goddess art and studies internationally, and has done many slide shows of her art and exhibitions with other women artists. She is also part of the women's spirituality movement, and is involved with paganism and earth mysteries.

INDEX